Good Luck!

"Technology continues to increase transparency and visibility into companies' business decisions, enabling transformation and driving competitive advantage. McAfee clearly understands the role of IT to create superior customer value. His straightforward approach and the frameworks presented in this book will help organizations derive maximum value from their investments."

—Léo Apotheker, CEO,
SAP AG

"Web 2.0 has opened a new frontier for coordinating work, presaging a revolution in innovation and productivity. Andrew McAfee's book provides the best guide yet to this new terrain. The wise executive will master it before the competition does."

—Erik Brynjolfsson,
professor at the MIT Sloan School of Management;
Director, MIT Center for Digital Business;
and coauthor of *Wired for Innovation*

"As businesses and organizations leverage the power of networked Web 2.0 technologies, we will see companies and countries drive the next significant phase of Internet productivity. In *Enterprise 2.0*, McAfee articulates the opportunities and the challenges that will require a shift in thinking, as well as new business models. This book is a valuable resource that underlines the importance of staying ahead of this market transition—or missing opportunities to capture the power of collaboration, new innovations, and operational efficiencies."

—John Chambers,
Chairman and CEO, Cisco

"With *Enterprise 2.0*, Andrew McAfee has identified a truly disruptive innovation. If you want to profit from it, read this book."

—Clayton Christensen, Robert and Jane Cizik
Professor of Business Administration,
Harvard Business School, and author of *The Innovator's Dilemma*

"Andrew McAfee is the king of Enterprise 2.0. He's written a book that is low on hype and high on business value. There is much to gain from exploring these participative technologies, and little to fear."

—Thomas H. Davenport,
President's Distinguished Professor of IT and Management,
Babson College, and coauthor of *Competing on Analytics*

"Afraid of anything and everything 2.0? This is the book for you. McAfee captures why it matters—and highlights case studies that demonstrate how you can make collaboration work for you. And I love that a government example is among the case studies. It is a must-read for those looking to gain their sea legs for the changing times ahead."

—Christopher Dorobek,
anchor on Federal News Radio 1500 AM,
Washington, D.C., and Editor in Chief, DorobekInsider.com

"McAfee combines enlightening anecdotes with in-depth case studies and sensible recommendations on how to think about and use Web 2.0 technologies in organizations. This book will persuade anyone skeptical of the value of Enterprise 2.0."

Irene Greif,
Director, Collaborative User Experience, IBM

"We are on the cusp of a management revolution that is likely to be as profound and unsettling as the one that gave birth to the modern industrial age. Driven by the emergence of powerful new collaborative technologies, this transformation will radically reshape the nature of work, the boundaries of the enterprise, and the responsibilities of business leaders. In *Enterprise 2.0,* Andrew McAfee delivers essential insights into the critical and fast-changing interface between IT and the organization. If you're intent on positioning your business for the future and would rather lead than follow, you need to read this book."

—Gary Hamel,
author of *Leading the Revolution* and *Competing for the Future*

"Andrew McAfee coined the term *Enterprise 2.0* to describe a phenomenon that has changed the way the world does business. Now he takes it a step further. Whether your firm is already deeply embedded in Enterprise 2.0 or you are trying to communicate its value to your staff and your customers, you will soon wear out this book by repeatedly referring to its thoughtful descriptions, advice, and insights."

—Paul F. Levy,
President and CEO, Beth Israel
Deaconess Medical Center

"This is an intensely practical book on what the Web 2.0 revolution is and what it means to managers. Highly readable, it succinctly describes the new technologies, what capabilities they can bring to an organization and their challenges of implementation. Whether or not you are familiar with Web 2.0, this book is a mandatory read."

—F. Warren McFarlan, Albert H. Gordon
Professor of Business Administration, Emeritus,
Harvard Business School

"Professor McAfee has written an important book for the true 'silent majority'—the hundreds of millions of workers globally who have had expensive technology dumped on their desks. Here he shows how non-IT managers can leverage a new wave of free, collaborative software that they actually enjoy using."

Bruce Richardson,
Chief Research Officer, AMR Research

"Andy McAfee spotted and shaped the trend toward Enterprise 2.0 early on and shows a clear perspective on where value will be created as this new wave of technology applications changes some of the long-standing rules of business. He very effectively keeps the focus not on the technologies themselves but rather on the implications for how executives will run their businesses in the future. The insights from his fieldwork provide today's business leaders with a pragmatic view of the opportunities and challenges these trends and technologies will create for their organizations."

—Roger Roberts,
Partner, McKinsey and Company, and leader of McKinsey's Business Technology Strategy service line in North America

ENTERPRISE 2.0

ENTERPRISE 2.0

NEW COLLABORATIVE TOOLS FOR YOUR ORGANIZATION'S TOUGHEST CHALLENGES

ANDREW MCAFEE

Harvard Business Press

Boston, Massachusetts

Library of Congress Cataloging-in-Publication Data

McAfee, Andrew.
  Enterprise 2.0 : new collaborative tools for your organization's toughest challenges / Andrew McAfee.
      p. cm.
  Includes bibliographical references and index.
  ISBN 978-1-4221-2587-8 (hbk. : alk. paper) 1.   Information technology—Management. 2.   Technological innovation—Management. 3.   Web 2.0. 4.   Online social networks. I.   Title.
  HD30.2.M387 2009
  658.4'038—dc22

                                                        2009019373

I know of no safe repository of the ultimate
power of society but people. And if we think them
not enlightened enough, the remedy is not to take
the power from them, but to inform them by education.

-Thomas Jefferson, in a 1787 letter to James Madison

To my parents, David and Nancy, for showing me the deep

joy inherent in both curiosity and hard work.

Contents

Acknowledgments   *ix*

1   Introduction   1

Part I   ENTERPRISE 2.0
The Power of Technology-Enabled Collaboration

2   Vexations and Missed
    Opportunities in Group Work   21
    Four Case Studies

3   Web 2.0 and the Emergence of Emergence   43
    A History, Explanation, and Definition of Enterprise 2.0

4   New Approaches to Old Problems   81
    Hitting the Bull's-Eye with Enterprise 2.0

5　Uniquely Valuable 129

The Benefits of Enterprise 2.0

Part II　SUCCEEDING WITH ENTERPRISE 2.0

6　Red Herrings and Long Hauls 145

*What Is, and Isn't, Difficult About Adopting
the New Tools and Approaches*

7　Going Mainstream 173

A Road Map for Enterprise 2.0 Success

8　Looking Ahead 195

*The Vision, the Liar's Club, and Model 1 Versus
Model 2 Behavior*

Notes 215
Index 221
About the Author 231

Acknowledgments

If you want to find out who your friends are, dump a book-length manuscript into the laps of a bunch of people and say, "Could you read this for me?" My mother, Nancy Haller, and my brother, David McAfee, took time out of their busy lives to do just that, and both read carefully and provided feedback above and beyond the call of shared DNA. My brother amazed me with his helpfulness; in the middle of preparing to move his family to Madagascar, he sequestered himself for a couple days and emerged with a set of extremely sharp comments and edits.

My great friend Anna Ivey did the same, applying her gift for clear thinking and formidable editing and proofreading skills to my initial draft. A first-time author is a sensitive and easily wounded soul, and Anna was as gentle with my ego as she was firm with my ideas and prose. I will be forever grateful to her.

Brian Surette was my editor at Harvard Business Press, and was a great colleague at every stage from conceptualizing this book to preparing it for the market. He was particularly insightful at seeing how the initial draft should be reshaped so that it flowed better, seeing possibilities that had never occurred to me. Monica Jainschigg whipped the manuscript into shape, and Jeff Kehoe was the first person from the Press to approach me about turning my initial *Sloan Management Review* article on Enterprise 2.0 into a book. I am grateful to all of them, and to the three reviewers who encouraged improvement and publication of the book.

The ideas that wound up on the pages here were, for the most part, initiated and stress-tested on my blog, in MBA and executive education classrooms, and in front of audiences at many conferences and seminars. I'm grateful to the people who participated in these forums by asking questions, voicing objections and concerns, and engaging with me on the subject matter. I can only hope that they learned as much as I did. I'd also like to thank David Streiff of Harvard Business School's IT staff, who set up and maintained my initial blog, thereby allowing me to practice what I preached about emergent social software platforms.

The field research that led to the case studies opening this book was supported by the HBS Department of Research and conducted in collaboration (at various times) with Karim Lakhani, Peter Coles, and Anders Sjoman, all of whom were fantastic colleagues. So was my faculty assistant, Esther Simmons, who by now is the only hope for getting me to show up at the right place and time. Thank you, Esther, for never losing patience with me.

I want to offer special thank-you's to Ross Mayfield, founder of enterprise wiki vendor SocialText, and JP Rangaswami, who was the CIO of the investment bank DrKW when I did my case study interviews there. I feel like they introduced me to the world of Enterprise 2.0 and helped me understand why it was worthy of attention and study. I met both Ross and JP through my student Matthew Mahoney, who came into my office one day in 2004 and announced that he wanted to do his course project on wikis. I replied that I liked *Star Wars* too, but that the movie's creatures weren't really appropriate for study at the MBA level. He explained that he was not, in fact, referring to Chewbacca, and started talking to me about a fascinating new technology for collaboration. That conversation led directly, if not immediately, to this book. So thanks, Matt.

1

Introduction

Skinheads are behind this book.

Before I explain how and why this is, let me talk a bit about this book and its goals. It's a book about how businesses are using a new set of technologies that appeared over the past few years on the Internet. To many people, these tools seemed so novel and important that they merited a whole new version number for the Web; *Web 2.0* was created to describe them, and to highlight their impact on the Internet.

I coined the term *Enterprise 2.0* to describe how these same technologies could be used on organizations' intranets and extranets, and to convey the impact they would have on business. This book is devoted to that topic. It has four main purposes. First, it's an overview and description of a bunch of new and (to many people) strange technologies and technology-based communities: blogs, Facebook, Wikipedia, Twitter, wikis, prediction markets, the PageRank algorithm, Delicious, social networking software, and others. It'll describe what each is, concentrating not on its technical details but instead on what it's used for—what tasks it accomplishes and what needs it's designed to fill. If you've heard about these entities but aren't sure what they are and what purpose they serve, these descriptions should be valuable.

Second, and much more importantly, I'll show that these technologies are not simply a random assortment. Though they do differ in significant ways, they also all share some deep similarities, similarities that make them all part of the same broad trend. As I'll describe in chapter 3, this trend is the use of technology to bring people together and let them interact, without specifying how they should do so. While this sounds like a recipe for chaos, it's actually just the opposite; the technologies of Web 2.0 and Enterprise 2.0 have the wonderful property of causing patterns and structure to appear over time, even though they're not specified up front.

Third, this book will illustrate how companies and other organizations are applying these technologies to critically important areas. I'll use case studies, supported with both well-established theories and new frameworks, to show how and where the tools of Enterprise 2.0 are being deployed and generating results. These examples will show how leaders are applying new tools, new approaches, and new philosophies to challenges such as accurately predicting the future (in domains where traditional forecasting methods have a poor track record); creating, gathering, and sharing knowledge; increasing rates of innovation; locating answers and expertise; and identifying and solving problems more quickly. For most organizations that I'm familiar with, these issues are not peripheral; they're central. I know that the subtitle of this book—*New Collaborative Tools for Your Organization's Toughest Challenges*—is a bold one, but I honestly believe it's warranted. The tools and techniques described in this book can help you with some of your most vexing problems (and I make that claim without knowing anything about your organization!).

The fourth and final purpose of this book is to provide guidance about how to succeed with Enterprise 2.0. As we'll see, it is not enough simply to deploy the new technologies of interaction and collaboration and then sit back and wait for the benefits to accrue. That strategy will almost certainly lead to disappointment and failure. I'll present a road map for success, concentrating on the roles played by business leaders—managers and executives outside the IT department. These leaders are the most important constituency for successful use of the newly available technologies of Enterprise 2.0; this book will reveal why this is, and how and where business leaders can most effectively intervene in order to gain access to the benefits offered by these tools.

Now, about those skinheads. They're behind this book because they helped me overcome my deep initial skepticism about the new tools and the communities built on top of them.

I'm not a skeptic about information technology in general. I've been studying IT's impact on how businesses perform and how they compete since 1994, when I started my doctorate at Harvard Business School. And one thing that's clear from a large and growing body of research is that IT as a rule significantly enhances productivity. Technology helps a company do more with less. What's more, IT helps companies keep doing even more with even less, year after year. In other words, it doesn't just offer productivity benefits at one point in time, but keeps offering them over time.

This sustained benefit is due in part to the incredible rates of invention and innovation in the high-tech sector—the hardware, software, networking, and Internet industries. As part of my research I tried to familiarize myself with this fascinating sector of the economy. If I was going to try to understand how technology is consumed, I reasoned, I had better also understand something about how it is produced.

I came to two broad conclusions about the technology-producing industries. First, they are hotbeds of innovation. They turn out new offerings at an astonishing pace, many of which are profoundly novel and beneficial. My off-the-top-of-the-head list of important new technologies that have appeared just during my own academic career includes Web browsers, PDAs, XML, modern Enterprise Resource Planning (ERP) systems, RSS, the Blackberry, the iPod and iPhone, Java, wikis, and Google's PageRank algorithm. Large and influential companies, many of them founded since the mid-1990s, have either generated or profited from these innovations. A quick list of such companies includes Amazon, eBay, Google, SAP, Oracle, Cisco, Microsoft, Salesforce.com, Apple, Facebook, and RIM.

Most of these technologies and companies were as distant as Neptune when I was an undergraduate at a very tech-friendly school (MIT) only twenty five years ago. Whenever I stand still and look back over the history of the high-tech sector, I am simply astonished at the pace and volume of innovation.

My second conclusion about this sector, though, is less positive. I've noticed that technology producers and the industries that surround them are at least as good at talking about innovation as they are at actually innovating. The vendors themselves carry on a constant monologue about their latest offerings, and about the even further advances that will be incorporated into their next versions. This monologue is echoed and amplified by a set of "helper industries" that include marketing and public relations companies, trade publications, and technology analysts. Without questioning the objectivity of any of these functions, it's fair to say that none of them is really in the business of telling their audience, "There's nothing new here" or, "Things are relatively quiet at present" or, "We believe that this trend is largely hype and can safely be ignored." Instead, their interests are largely aligned with those of the vendors; they all have a stake in portraying the high-tech sector as ceaselessly interesting and innovative, and one that can't be safely ignored even for a short time.

In the early years of the new millennium I found myself much less willing to accept this image of high-tech industries, simply because it had so clearly been wrong in important instances. Many of the key segments of the "new economy," including consumer Internet portals and B2B exchanges, had collapsed entirely during the dot-com meltdown, and in retrospect the volume of uncritical enthusiasm and praise for these businesses seems bizarre. Similarly, the dire warnings in the late 1990s about the looming "Y2K crisis" were clearly overblown, often to the point of absurdity: the *Wired* magazine cover story for April 1999, for example, stated that, "Whatever the Y2K crisis turns out to be, it is already unprecedented: We have never before anticipated the simultaneous breakdown of a significant fraction of the world's machinery . . . maybe, just maybe, a lot of things—say, most things—will fall apart. Contrary to what the Social Security Administration has promised, pensioners in the US won't get their Social Security checks after all, but that won't matter much, because we won't have a financial system that knows what to do with checks."[1]

As it turned out, the Y2K crisis was not averted because all companies fixed every line of code that contained a two-digit

year; it was averted because there was not much of a crisis to
begin with.

So I resolved in the early years of the millennium not to
buy the tech sector's hype, and instead to be skeptical of its
claims of constant novelty. When I started to hear talk of
"Web 2.0," then, I was immediately on guard. The phrase made
the extraordinary claim that a new version number for the Web
was warranted—that instead of incremental improvements, a
great leap forward had taken place, and that a new World Wide
Web was out there.

"Oh, give it a rest, would you?" I thought to myself.

When I first started hearing "Web 2.0" I was studying corporate technologies rather than consumer ones, and didn't really want to switch. In fact, I wanted to spend as little time as
possible investigating Web 2.0 because I was so convinced that
it was nothing more than a new marketing buzzphrase invented
by a vendor or member of one of the helper industries, and that
it was yet another example of the tech sector's tendency to put
old wine in new bottles. I felt I needed to familiarize myself
with Web 2.0, if for no other reason than to say to my MBA and
executive education students that they could (and should)
ignore it. Essentially, I just wanted to confirm my jaundiced
hypothesis and move on.

So I fired up Wikipedia and thought about which of its articles to look at first. By early 2005 Wikipedia was receiving large
amounts of media attention, and was often held up as a prime
example of Web 2.0. Which, I thought, made this the perfect
time to watch it break down. I knew from my cursory reading
that Wikipedia was a collaboratively produced, highly egalitarian encyclopedia. Virtually anyone could start a new article, edit
an existing one, or reject someone else's edits. I believed that

although this approach was commendable in many ways, it was also doomed, especially as the number of people aware of Wikipedia mushroomed.

I knew enough about the history of online communities, both from my reading and from firsthand experience in Usenet groups, to know that they usually don't scale well. This failing is especially true if they're open to everyone and inherently utopian—based on the assumption that all members will work together with good will and in good faith. Reality is unpleasant to such communities because some people don't work this way: they post spam, spew hate speech and other vile content, bait other members into endless arguments, and generally act in ways that decrease the value of the community for other members.

Even a small number of members who act negatively can greatly harm an online community, and most communities attract such members as they grow. The two most common responses to their presence are to appoint gatekeepers to review all contributions before they appear online, or to close the community, that is, to impose entry criteria and keep many people out. Yet I knew from my initial reading that Wikipedia had taken neither of these steps. It had remained radically open, even as it grew to be quite large and well publicized.

So in early 2005 I thought that Wikipedia must be breaking down in predictable ways. I visited the site for the first time with the goal of watching this breakdown take place and then moving on to other things (or, to be honest, going back to previous things). To accomplish this goal, the first word I typed into Wikipedia's search box was *skinhead*.

I have a shaved head, but it's not a political statement; I'm not a skinhead. In fact, I knew almost nothing about skinheads at the time. I had heard, though, that there are two broad categories of skinhead. The first is the type that most of us are all too aware of: the violent, racist jingoists, often neo-Nazi, who stomp on immigrants in their leisure hours. The second category consists of people who have very similar haircuts and clothes (at least to the untrained eye), but exactly the opposite political philosophy; these skinheads practice and preach love, tolerance, and racial equality.

This surface-level knowledge of skinheads convinced me that the Wikipedia page devoted to them would be a great place to watch this online encyclopedia come apart. I thought that if hate speech and venomous arguments would be especially visible, nasty, and counterproductive anywhere, it would be on that page. I typed the word *skinhead*, hit "Go," and sat back to enjoy the fireworks.

I was taken to an article that began, "Skinheads, named after their shaven heads, are members of a subculture that originated in Britain in the 1960s, where they were closely tied to the Rude boys of the West Indies and the Mods of the UK."[2]

Contents

- 1 Categories

    o 1.1 In-fighting and Hostilities

- 2 History

- 3 Style

    o 3.1 Laces & Braces

- 4 Music

- 5 Glossary of terms

- 6 See Also

- 7 External Links

The article was over twenty-five hundred words long, and although in places it was roughly written and edited, it was the best short summary of all things skinhead I had come across. It was concise, informative, objective, apparently thorough, and extensively referenced—everything a good encyclopedia article should be. Nowhere in the text of the article did I see arguments, hate speech, or flame wars break out. Instead, I saw Wikipedia working as advertised in an area where I had expected to see just the opposite.

After I finished reading the article, I said to myself, "There's something new under the sun here" and began to suspect that Web 2.0 was in fact not just blind hype—that it was in fact useful shorthand for what was then taking place on the Internet.

However, I'm not interested in the Internet for its own sake, and my research doesn't center on the Web, virtual communities, or online business models. I'm fascinated by the Internet, Moore's Law, Metcalfe's Law, and the Network Era (who wouldn't be?), but I'm even more interested in how companies in "boring" industries deploy and exploit technology to do exciting things—things that make their executives and shareholders happy. In short, I'm more interested in how technology is consumed than in how it is produced.

My research also doesn't focus on entrepreneurs, venture capitalists, coders, or CIOs. These are all vitally important constituencies in the tech sector and I interact with all of them. I'm most interested, however, in what technology means for line managers, those people responsible for developing valuable offerings, getting them out the door, and getting paid for them.

These managers have frequently been left out of IT discussions, which in my view is a serious mistake. I believe that general managers are the single most important constituency for technology success or failure within an organization; yet very few books or other materials are written especially for them.

This book is an attempt to fill that gap. It summarizes the work I've done over the past few years to understand what recent developments on the Internet mean for corporate intranets and extranets, to describe the exciting new capabilities offered by these novel technologies, and to identify how best to harness their power. It's written for general managers, and as such it assumes little to no prior familiarity with the technologies it covers.

This book has one broad message for this audience: the story of how businesses use technology is about to become a lot more interesting.

After the Y2K "crisis" passed and the Internet stock bubble burst in the spring of 2000, the tech sector calmed down for a while. Companies continued to spend money on hardware, software, and networks, of course, but it seemed as if the toolkit of information technologies available to help businesses accomplish their goals was largely stable, and no longer changing as quickly as it had been doing.

For many people, this stability was welcome. The late 1990s were a time of incredible technology innovation and change, and decision makers both inside and outside IT departments frequently felt overwhelmed. Executives and managers were confronted with the Internet and the Web; eCommerce and eBusiness; large-scale enterprise systems such as ERP, Customer Relationship Management, and Supply Chain Management, and the looming threat that everything would stop working on January 1, 2000.

These developments were particularly unsettling, not only because they appeared so suddenly and in such rapid succession but also because they were all related to IT, a domain well outside the comfort zone of most business decision makers. For many, if not most, managers the world of technology—which includes IT departments, equipment and software vendors, and specialized consultants and analysts—is a closed one. Its members seem almost to speak a different language, and to be in some ways hostile to outsiders. It's easy to believe that it would require years of study and apprenticeship to break into the world of IT. Since the mid-1990s I've taught hundreds of business executives, and they have often displayed levels of "tech anxiety" that remind me of high school students' math anxiety.

Still, these executives tried. In the late 1990s managers in virtually every industry made sincere efforts to educate themselves about the newly available technologies and their impact on business practices and competitive strategies. They also invested significant amounts of time, money, and effort in deploying the new tools and harnessing their power. Many of these efforts were perceived as successes, but many others weren't. So the calmer environment of the first years of the new century was welcomed by many managers and companies in technology-consuming industries. It meant that they had less to absorb, understand, and deploy.

An article about corporate IT in the May 2003 issue of *Harvard Business Review* was also welcomed in many quarters, although it was also widely derided. Written by HBR editor-at-large Nicholas Carr, it was titled simply "IT Doesn't Matter." Carr's argument was straightforward: IT, he wrote, was "becoming [a cost] of doing business that must be paid by all but provide[s] distinction to none." Because of this commoditization,

"the greatest IT risk facing most companies is . . . overspend-
ing" and "IT management should, frankly, become boring."[3]
Carr's article and subsequent book on the same topic were, to
put it mildly, not well received in the high-tech sector, but they
found many receptive readers within organizations that had invested heavily in IT but remained uncertain as to what they had
received in return.

In this environment of lower spending and lowered expectations, few people anticipated the appearance of a new and
powerful set of information technologies for corporations
(I know I didn't). And even fewer were expecting that these
new digital tools would originate not in a university research
center or lab at Microsoft, IBM, SAP, or Oracle, but rather in a
group of online collaborative communities, some of which were
explicitly not for profit.

Yet this is what happened. A suite of technologies developed to support communities on the Web is entering companies and having a large impact on them. This book aims to
describe these tools, show why and where their impact will be
felt, and offer advice and guidance to decision makers about
how to select and deploy them effectively.

In a spring 2006 article in the journal *Sloan Management Review* I introduced the term *Enterprise 2.0* as shorthand for the use
of Web 2.0 technologies by businesses in pursuit of their goals.[4]
It caught on, and is now in fairly common use. At about the
same time the article appeared, I started a blog about my work,
and most of my blog posts have been about Enterprise 2.0.

So is this book. Although it's about IT, it's not written for
programmers, systems analysts, CIOs, gadget freaks, or other
technophiles. Rather, it's written for businesspeople, in particular the managers and executives responsible for setting and

achieving their organization's goals. If you're part of this population of business decision makers, I hope to show you that no
matter what industry you're in, the new technologies I'll describe can be highly beneficial and help you address longstand-
ing challenges in new ways. I also hope to show that no matter
what kind of organization you're part of—young or old, big or
small, cutting-edge or mainstream—these new technologies are
accessible and appropriate, as are the new approaches to collaboration and interaction that make use of them. As we'll see, the
phenomenon I call Enterprise 2.0—business use of the new tools
of collaboration—is not confined to "new economy" companies,
nor to those full of Gen Y workers: the benefits of Enterprise 2.0
are available to any organization.

These benefits, however, are not automatic. Experience
shows that it's surprisingly difficult for people and organizations
to move away from their current collaborative tools and habits
and adopt new ones. Managers must involve themselves in this
transition if they want it to be successful, and the chapters that
follow show where, when, and how they can most effectively
intervene.

This book should also be useful and relevant to other
groups involved in developing IT and deploying it within organizations. High-tech vendors and entrepreneurs, consultants
and analysts, and of course people working within corporate IT
departments should find its topics worthwhile and its content
informative.

The content is divided into two parts: part I explains what
Enterprise 2.0 is and why it's valuable, while part II offers guidance for managers about how to deploy the new tools and practices of collaboration successfully. Chapter 2 kicks off part I
by presenting four recent case studies of organizations facing

familiar challenges; these case studies are not resolved in the chapter, but instead left hanging. Chapter 3 then takes a short step backward in time to describe how a group of new collaborative technologies and communities appeared on the Internet over the past few years; this chapter stresses how these were not just incremental improvements over what was in place before, but were instead radical departures that addressed the shortcomings of previous approaches. Chapter 4 then returns to the case studies, discussing how each of the organizations adopted new technologies and collaborative practices and benefited greatly from them. This chapter also places the case studies within a broader framework that illustrates the value of Enterprise 2.0 for four different categories of user: strongly tied colleagues (in other words, close ones), weakly tied colleagues, potential collaborators who are not yet working together, and "professional strangers." Chapter 5 concludes part I by discussing the concrete business benefits provided by successful Enterprise 2.0 deployments.

Part II explains how to successfully apply the new technologies of collaboration and the work practices that make use of them. Chapter 6 begins by listing the most common concerns that deter organizations and their leaders from embarking on an Enterprise 2.0 effort. These concerns appear daunting at first, but experience and evidence reveal that they're actually not insurmountable—and that most of them are not serious impediments at all. This chapter then shows how the most serious barrier to Enterprise 2.0 is the unwillingness of many individuals to give up their existing collaborative tools and practices, even though these are clearly inferior in important ways, and reveals the deep-seated reasons for this reluctance. Chapter 7 builds on this understanding to offer both technologists and general managers guidelines for overcoming this hesitation and succeeding in the use of Enterprise 2.0 initiatives. These guidelines apply to both technologists and general managers. Chapter 8 concludes the book by making some grounded projections about the future of collaborative work, taking into account both the largest threats and the greatest opportunities associated with the tools now available.

The story of how businesses use technology is about to get much more interesting because Enterprise 2.0 offers significant improvements, not just incremental ones, in areas such as generating, capturing, and sharing knowledge; letting people find helpful colleagues; tapping into new sources of innovation and expertise; and harnessing the "wisdom of crowds." These are critical activities, yet many organizations feel that they're currently stumbling rather than excelling at them. There's also a widespread perception that the technologies currently in place to support these activities are weak, primitive, and unpopular.

Because of Enterprise 2.0, this situation is already changing at some organizations. As the case studies and examples in the chapters that follow illustrate, leading companies are deploying the new tools of collaboration and interaction; changing established norms, practices, and processes; and reaping rewards. As the science fiction writer William Gibson observed, "The future is already here—it's just not evenly distributed." Case studies of early adopters offer us a glimpse of Enterprise 2.0's exciting future, and this book includes case studies of organizations as different as Google and the CIA.

The adjective *social* is often applied to the technologies discussed in this book. This label is accurate, but unfortunate. When some managers hear talk of social technologies, they immediately think of technologies that facilitate activities like happy hour, fantasy sports league drafts, and office gossip. They hear "social," in short, and think it means not work-related, or time-wasting, or productivity-draining.

Because of this tendency, I rarely if ever use the word *social* when discussing Enterprise 2.0. I prefer instead *collaborative*, a term that has largely positive connotations for business leaders. People collaborate in order to get work done and solve problems, and these days there's no shortage of problems to solve. As I write (in early 2009), the worldwide economy is beset by a severe recession, and companies must figure out how to keep innovating and pleasing their customers while at the same time slashing costs and improving efficiency.

This is a daunting task, and it makes great sense to harness all available brainpower for it. As the open source software proponent Eric Raymond says about fixing computer programs, "With enough eyeballs all bugs are shallow." With enough brains, many, if not most, business challenges can be met, and Enterprise 2.0 is all about using technology to bring brains together effectively. Now more than ever, this seems a smart thing for organizations to be doing.

One more note on terminology. My professional home is a business school, so the bulk of my research has been conducted in the private sector rather than within government and non-profit agencies. As a result, I more often use the nouns *business* and *company* and the adjective *corporate* rather than the broader terms *organization* and *organizational*. I don't mean to imply, though, that Enterprise 2.0 is limited to the private sector, or that it should be. All of this book's content is applicable to both public and private organizations, and I hope readers from outside the corporate world will forgive me for frequently talking about "companies."

I also hope that as a result of reading this book you'll join the ongoing conversation around Enterprise 2.0. I participate in this discussion via my blog (andrewmcafee.org/blog), my Facebook profile (www.facebook.com/amcafee), and my Twitter identity @amcafee. If you don't yet know what blogs, Facebook, or Twitter are, don't worry; they're all explained in the pages that follow. Sign up, subscribe, leave a comment, send a message, and just generally join in on my emergent social software platforms (another term explained in the text). You'll find that it's a great way to educate yourself about Enterprise 2.0. I look forward to hearing from you.

No one is more surprised than I am by this book. I had no plan a few years ago to investigate any new Internet technologies or online communities, and certainly no idea that I would make use of the "2.0" suffix myself. The only credit I give myself is for being just open-minded enough to test my initial skepticism about Web 2.0. The rest, I guess, I owe to skinheads . . .

Part I

ENTERPRISE 2.0

The Power of Technology-Enabled Collaboration

2

Vexations and Missed Opportunities in Group Work

Four Case Studies

W e'll begin this chapter with four short case studies that have come out of my recent research. Three of them are about companies; the fourth is about a government entity. Two of them concern large organizations; the other two deal with small ones. Two are set within the high-tech sector; two are not. And in three cases a problem has been identified, while in the fourth someone senses a new opportunity.

In short, these four stories are dissimilar. In addition to covering different types of organizations, they also present a wide range of issues: capturing and sharing knowledge, building corporate culture, training new employees in a rapidly growing company, putting people in touch with each other across a large and fragmented enterprise, tapping into the "wisdom of crowds," and giving people easier, faster, and better access to the information they need to do their jobs well.

So what, if anything, do these stories have in common? They share three characteristics. First, they all focus on group-level work and interactions among knowledge workers. Second, they're all left unresolved in this chapter. I apologize in advance for leaving you hanging in this way and promise to return to each of these four stories later in the book.

The third common element in these case studies, as you've probably guessed, is information technology. As we'll see later, technology is used to resolve each of the four situations presented in this chapter. The "right" technology may not be obvious in each case—in fact, I hope it's not—but each organization effectively addresses its challenges and opportunities by deploying and using IT.

What's more, the technologies deployed in all cases are novel ones. Most of them weren't available even ten years ago. The story of how they came to be, and why they are ideally suited for business needs like those presented here, is the story of this book. An important aspect of this story is understanding why previous generations of technology designed to facilitate collaboration within organizations were not well suited for the situations described here. I'll discuss that issue after presenting the case studies.

I've arranged these four stories in a deliberate order. The first concerns a relatively small group of people who work together closely. The second focuses on a larger group of people in many locations who all work at the same company, but don't know each other well. The third is about an even larger population of knowledge workers spread across several organizations who should be sharing information and expertise, but are not doing so. And the fourth and final case study encompasses all the employees of one big company, most of whom will never need to work together.

In each successive example, the strength of the professional relationships between the people involved decreases, moving from close colleagues in the first case to professional strangers in the fourth. I chose this progression for two reasons. First, it illustrates the impressive flexibility and applicability of Enterprise 2.0 tools, which we'll see are useful not just in one or two of these situations, but in every one of them. Second, this sequence reveals a useful framework for understanding the benefits of Enterprise 2.0 that is based on a great deal of existing research and theory and can be applied to almost any situation. This framework uses the concept of tie strength among knowledge workers, that is, the closeness and depth of their professional relationships. As we'll see in chapter 3, this concept of tie strength reveals the power of Enterprise 2.0, as well as its breadth. The new tools of collaboration and interaction provide benefits to close colleagues, professional strangers, and every level of tie strength in between. Before describing these benefits, though, let's look at our four real-world problems, challenges, and missed opportunities.

VistaPrint

By 2008, VistaPrint was becoming a victim of its own success. The company, which was founded in 1995 within the already-crowded direct marketing industry for printed products, initially differentiated itself with a compelling offer to consumers: it gave

away business cards free to anyone who wanted them. Visitors to
www.vistaprint.com could obtain 250 business cards for the cost
of shipping only. Even though these cards were free, they did not
look cheap or generic. People could customize them by selecting
from a range of templates and logos, and they were printed on
high-quality paper. The free cards helped to spread the word
about the company, with the tagline "Business cards are free
at www.vistaprint.com" printed in small type on the back of
each one. By 2008 the company had given away over three
billion cards.

VistaPrint used technology extensively to keep costs low
while giving away large amounts of free merchandise. Company
engineers modified the presses used to print business cards and
other materials to make them more flexible. They also wrote
programs that "looked at" the stream of incoming orders and
determined which ones to print together in order to minimize
waste. This combination of hardware and software allowed
VistaPrint to receive a large number of small orders online, combine them on the fly into optimal configurations, and print
them as cheaply as possible.

If customers wanted only free merchandise, however,
VistaPrint was not going to stay in business for very long. The
company became proficient at the practice of *up-selling*, that is,
persuading customers to pay a small amount for a product they
perceived to be superior. For business cards, this might mean
higher-quality paper, more colors, or greater freedom to choose
a logo or arrange the card's elements. VistaPrint learned what
customers were willing to pay for these options and priced its
products accordingly. Experience showed that even customers
who originally intended to take advantage of free cards might
wind up spending $10 or $20 in order to get "better" ones.

Because of VistaPrint's highly efficient operations, such small orders could be produced profitably.

If customers were satisfied with their initial orders, they often returned to the Web site and purchased additional products. Over time VistaPrint expanded into a wide range of additional paper products—presentation folders, letterhead, notepads, postcards, calendars, sticky notes, brochures, and return address labels. The company also began to carry products such as pens, hats, T-shirts, car door magnets, lawn signs, and window decals. After initially targeting individuals, VistaPrint eventually came to market its products and services to "microbusinesses" employing fewer than ten people, offering them design, copywriting, and mailing services.

VistaPrint grew rapidly, and without making any acquisitions. By 2008 the company had revenues of $400 million and employed fourteen hundred people in six locations in North America, the Caribbean, and Europe. The Lexington, Massachusetts, office housed most of the executive team: the marketing, human resources, and finance functions and the teams responsible for IT, technology operations, and capabilities development.

The company had to hire many engineers and technology support personnel in Lexington to support its rapid growth. In the summer of 2007, for example, VistaPrint recruited more than twenty new software engineers, most of them recent college graduates. Since the department had employed only about sixty engineers up to this time, managers were concerned about how to integrate the large number of new hires smoothly without burdening the existing workforce too much, and without jeopardizing anything that the company had already built. VistaPrint had a large and complex code base (the interlinked applications that supported the company's operations), and it

would be easy for a new hire to inadvertently harm or destabi-
lize it by not following proper procedures. As Dan Barrett, a
senior software engineering manager, joked, "We need to train
our new people quickly so they don't break our software."[1]

Ideally, VistaPrint would have an easily consultable and
comprehensive reference work for new employees, but such a resource would be time-consuming to develop. It could also quickly
become outdated, since the company's technology changed so
rapidly. VistaPrint had a shared hard drive on which people saved
documentation and other reference work, but most people felt
that it was disorganized and hard to search. As at most companies, new employees at VistaPrint learned about the organization
and their jobs by observing their colleagues and asking lots of
questions.

Barrett, however, wondered if it were possible to do better
in this area. He was concerned about the challenges VistaPrint
faced not only when a new employee entered the company but
also when an experienced worker left it. Departing workers typically left little behind, especially in a form that could be easily
accessed or searched by others. This absence of records struck
him as a shame. Barrett also wondered how the company could
do a better job of sharing its accumulated knowledge and the
good ideas that were developed at each location. He felt that
many of the company's innovations and insights were not
shared widely enough; people at the Netherlands printing facil-
ity, for example, often faced problems that had already been
confronted and resolved at the sister site in Canada. Engineers
at the two locations talked to one another and sent e-mails frequently, of course, but Barrett and others had the impression
that people at VistaPrint were still doing a fair amount of redun-
dant work and "reinventing the wheel."

For VistaPrint, a relatively small company in the printing industry, managing growth and training new employees had become major challenges. How could the company capture its own engineering knowledge and deliver it to all new hires so that they could become productive as quickly as possible? And how could VistaPrint possibly ensure that this body of knowledge would remain current even as the company and its environment continued to change?

Serena Software

In 2007, Serena Software CEO Jeremy Burton felt that his company needed to make two fundamental shifts. First, it had to make a major addition to its product family. Up to that time, Serena had been an enterprise software company that helped its customers manage all of their enterprise software. Large organizations typically have many different pieces of enterprise software from different vendors; each of these applications is configured, and most are modified. In addition, software vendors release bug fixes, upgrades, and new versions over time. As a result, large organizations maintain highly complex software environments with many moving parts.

Serena's products, which fell into the category of Application Lifecycle Management software, helped its customers keep track of all these moving parts and the linkages and dependencies among them. The company had been founded more than twenty-five years earlier during the mainframe era of corporate computing and still offered mainframe products in 2007. It also developed and sold applications for software change and configuration management and project and portfolio management. Serena supplied over ninety-five of the *Fortune* 100 companies.

Burton and other executives wanted the company to enter the nascent market for software that helped companies build "mashups," that is, combinations of two or more existing enterprise systems and their data. Mashups were becoming very popular on the Internet as companies like Google "opened up" their applications, allowing virtually anyone to use and extend popular programs without requiring up-front permission. People did not need deep programming skills for this task; they could mash up Google Maps, for example, by combining its mapping capabilities with other data. One of the most popular early mashups on the Web was Chicago Crime, a mashup of Google Maps with crime data published by the Chicago Police Department; Chicago Crime allowed residents to look at crime patterns in their neighborhoods.[2]

In one way mashups were a logical extension of Serena's enterprise software capabilities, but in another sense they constituted a radical departure from the company's existing products. Mashups were a stereotypical Web 2.0 technology: they empowered individuals, heightened their ability to act autonomously, and increased information openness, transparency, and sharing. Corporate mashups, in essence, were about letting go of centralized control over enterprise IT. Serena's other offerings and its entire prior history, in contrast, emphasized maintaining control.

The company's employees had not grown up in the mashup era; many of them, in fact, had acquired their technical skills and started their careers well before the Web was born. The average age of Serena employees was approximately forty-five, and many were significantly older. These people had deep technical skills, but Burton wondered whether they were immersed enough in Web 2.0 tools and philosophies to develop great software for corporate mashups.

He also worried that whether or not they knew Web 2.0 well enough, they might not know *one another* well enough. Unlike VistaPrint, Serena had not just grown organically; it had made multiple acquisitions over the years, many of them in other countries. By 2007 the company had over eight hundred employees in eighteen countries. More than 35 percent of these people worked from home, giving them little if any opportunity to interact with their colleagues face to face.

Many at Serena were concerned that if the company continued on its current path, it could lose all sense of community and become little more than a collection of people all over the world who worked on projects together in virtual teams and earned paychecks. As vice president Kyle Arteaga explained it, "There was little sense of a Serena community. People often worked together for more than a decade, yet knew nothing about each other. There was no easy way to learn more about your colleagues because we had no shared space. We had all these home workers, or employees in satellite offices like Melbourne who we only knew by name."[3]

The second fundamental shift Burton was contemplating was a deliberate attempt to increase Serena's sense of community. But how was he to do so with such a patched-together and globally distributed workforce?

The U.S. Intelligence Community

In the wake of the September 11, 2001, terrorist attacks on the United States, several groups investigated the performance of the country's intelligence agencies, and did not like much of what they saw. Their conclusions can be summarized using two phrases that became popular during the investigations: even though the system was blinking red before 9/11, no one could connect the dots.

In an interview with the National Commission on Terrorist Attacks Upon the United States, better known as the 9/11 Commission, CIA director George Tenet maintained that "the system was blinking red" in the months before the attacks. In other words, there were ample warnings, delivered at the highest levels of government during the summer of 2001, that Osama bin Laden and his Al Qaeda operatives were planning large-scale attacks, perhaps within the United States. In some cases these warnings were frighteningly accurate: CIA analysts, for example, prepared a section titled "Bin Laden Determined to Strike in US" for the President's Daily Brief of August 6, 2001.[4]

These warnings were accurate and urgent in part because diverse actors scattered throughout the sixteen agencies that made up the U.S. intelligence community (IC) were convinced of the grave threat posed by Al Qaeda and dogged in their pursuit of this enemy. At the CIA, for example, a group called Alec Station, headed by Michael Scheuer, was dedicated to neutralizing bin Laden. At the FBI, counterterrorism chief Paul O'Neill and his team had gained firsthand experience of Islamic terrorists during investigations of attacks in Saudi Arabia and Yemen, and were determined not to let them strike in the United States again (in 1993 the World Trade Center had been attacked with a truck bomb). Richard Clarke, the chief counterterrorism adviser on the U.S. National Security Council, was the highest-level champion of these efforts, devoting great energy to assessing and communicating the danger posed by bin Laden's group.[5]

In the months preceding 9/11 troubling signs were apparent to intelligence agents and analysts throughout the world. In the

United States, agent Ken Williams of the FBI's Phoenix office wrote a memo in July 2001 to the bureau's counterterrorism division highlighting an "effort by Osama bin Laden to send students to the US to attend civil aviation universities and colleges" and proposing a nationwide program of monitoring flight schools.[6] On July 5th Clarke assembled a meeting with representatives from many agencies—including the FBI, the Secret Service, the Coast Guard, and the Federal Aviation Authority—and told them, "Something really spectacular is going to happen here, and it's going to happen soon."[7] Zacarias Moussaoui was taken into custody by agents from the FBI's Minneapolis office in August 2001 and immediately recognized as a terrorist threat. The Minneapolis office requested a search warrant of Moussaoui's laptop and personal effects, citing the crime of "Destruction of aircraft or aircraft facilities."[8]

No one, however, was able to "connect the dots" between all these pieces of evidence and perceive the nature and timing of the coming attacks clearly enough to prevent them. Investigators concluded that a major reason for this failure was the lack of effective information sharing both within and across intelligence agencies. Information flows were often "stovepiped," that is, reports, cables, and other intelligence products were sent up and down narrow channels within an agency, usually following formal chains of command. If someone within a stovepipe decided that no more analysis or action was appropriate, the issue *and* the information associated with it typically went no further. There were few natural or easy ways for someone to take information, analysis, conclusions, or concerns outside the stovepipe and share them more broadly within the community.

These documented failures to act on and share information before 9/11 proved devastating. The Moussaoui search warrant request, for example, was not granted until after the attacks had taken place. Throughout 2001 agents at both the CIA and FBI were interested in the activities and whereabouts of several suspected terrorists, including Khalid al-Mihdhar and Nawaf al-Hazmi. CIA investigations revealed that Mihdhar held a U.S. visa, and that Hazmi had traveled to the United States in January 2000. This information was not widely disseminated within the IC at the time that it was collected, however, and was also not shared with FBI agents during a June 2001 meeting of representatives from the two agencies during the investigation of the October 2000 bombing of the USS *Cole* in Yemen. At the time of the meeting, Mihdhar was not on the State Department's TIPOFF watch list, which was intended to prevent terrorists from entering the United States. He arrived in the United States in July 2001, and both he and Hazmi participated in the September 11 attacks.[9]

The volume and gravity of these information-sharing failures led some to conclude that the 9/11 attacks could have been prevented. Because of what the 9/11 Commission called "good instinct" among a small group of collaborators across the FBI and CIA, both Mihdhar and Hazmi were added to the TIPOFF list on August 24. However, efforts then initiated to find them within the United States were not successful. The Commission's report concluded,

> We believe that if more resources had been applied and a significantly different approach taken, Mihdhar and Hazmi might have been found . . .
>
> Both Hazmi and Mihdhar could have been held for immigration violations or as material witnesses in the *Cole* bombing case. Investigation or interrogation of

them, and investigation of their travel and financial activities, could have yielded evidence of connections to other participants in the 9/11 plot. The simple fact of their detention could have derailed the plan. In any case, the opportunity did not arise.[10]

The 9/11 Commission made a number of recommendations for improving the IC. These included, predictably, better information sharing:

> We have already stressed the importance of intelligence analysis that can draw on all relevant sources of information. The biggest impediment to all-source analysis—to a greater likelihood of connecting the dots—is the human or systemic resistance to sharing information . . .
>
> In the 9/11 story, for example, we sometimes see examples of information that could be accessed—like the undistributed NSA information that would have helped identify Nawaf al Hazmi in January 2000. But someone had to ask for it. In that case, no one did. Or . . . the information is distributed, but in a compartmented channel. Or the information is available, and someone does ask, but it cannot be shared . . .
>
> We propose that information be shared horizontally, across new networks that transcend individual agencies . . .
>
> The current system is structured on an old mainframe, or hub-and-spoke, concept. In this older approach, each agency has its own database. Agency users send information to the database and then can retrieve it from the database.

A decentralized network model, the concept behind much of the information revolution, shares data horizontally too . . .

No one agency can do it alone. Well-meaning agency officials are under tremendous pressure to update their systems. Alone, they may only be able to modernize the stovepipes, not replace them.[11]

The 9/11 Commission also recommended the creation of a director of national intelligence with some level of authority over all sixteen federal agencies. This director, it was hoped, could encourage better coordination and lessen the degree of stovepiping within the community. According to the commission's final report, "[With] a new National Intelligence Director empowered to set common standards for information use throughout the community, and a secretary of homeland security who helps extend the system to public agencies and relevant private-sector databases, a government-wide initiative can succeed."[12]

The Intelligence Reform and Terrorism Prevention Act of 2004 created the office of the Director of National Intelligence (DNI). In an official statement to the U.S. Senate in 2007, J. Michael McConnell, the second director, discussed the need for a deep shift in philosophy and policy within the IC:

> "Our success in preventing future attacks depends
> upon our ability to gather, analyze, and share informa-
> tion and intelligence regarding those who would do us
> more harm . . . Most important, the long-standing pol-
> icy of only allowing officials access to intelligence on a
> "need to know" basis should be abandoned for a mind-
> set guided by a "responsibility to provide" intelligence

to policymakers, warfighters, and analysts, while still ensuring the protection of sources and methods."[13]

Not all observers, however, felt that the DNI would be able to accomplish much, or to effect deep change in the agencies' strong and entrenched cultures. The federal commission established to investigate the IC's poor performance in determining whether Iraq possessed weapons of mass destruction was particularly blunt. Its final report stated that "commission after commission has identified some of the same fundamental failings we see in the Intelligence Community, usually to little effect. The Intelligence Community is a closed world, and many insiders admitted to us that *it has an almost perfect record of resisting external recommendations*" (emphasis in original).[14] The journalist Fred Kaplan, writing in the online magazine *Slate*, was also pessimistic: "There will be a director of national intelligence. But the post will likely be a figurehead, at best someone like the chairman of the Council of Economic Advisers, at worst a thin new layer of bureaucracy . . . "[15]

Many wondered how a "thin new layer of bureaucracy" could possibly address the IC's inability to connect the dots, or start to change its deeply entrenched "need to know" culture. Could U.S. intelligence analysts ever learn to share what they knew and collaborate more effectively? What might encourage them to do so?

The IC decided to look within itself for answers to these questions. The DNI took over from the director of central intelligence (the head of the CIA) a novel program, called the Galileo Awards, intended to solicit innovative solutions to challenges facing the IC from community members themselves. The Galileo Awards' first call for papers went out in 2004.

Google

In June 2004, while on vacation from his job at Google, Bo Cowgill was seized by an idea that would not let go of him. He had gone to work for Google the previous year after finishing his bachelor's degree in public policy at Stanford. He liked the company, but hoped to move on from his entry-level customer support job.

One of the books he had taken with him on vacation was James Surowiecki's *The Wisdom of Crowds*.[16] The book's theme was that it was often possible to harness the "collective intelligence" of a group of people and thus yield better or more accurate information than any individual within the group possessed. Many readers found this a powerful and novel message. They were accustomed to thinking that groups usually yielded the "lowest common denominator" of their members' contributions or, even worse, that groups could turn into mobs that actually behaved less intelligently than *any* of their members.

The Wisdom of Crowds provided many examples of collective intelligence, including one that was familiar to Cowgill. He had learned as an undergraduate about the Iowa Electronic Markets (IEM), an ongoing experiment begun in 1988 at the University of Iowa that sought to test whether the same principles and tools that supported stock markets could be used to predict the results of political elections. The IEM and other similar environments came to be known as prediction markets.

Just like public stock markets, prediction markets are composed of securities, each of which has a price. People use the market to trade with one another by buying and selling these securities. Because traders have differing beliefs about what the securities are worth, and because events occur over time that alter these beliefs, the prices of securities vary over time in all markets.

In a stock market like the New York Stock Exchange the securities being traded are shares in companies, the price of which reflects beliefs about the value of their future profits. In a prediction market, in contrast, the securities being traded are related to future events such as a U.S. presidential election. In that case the market can be designed so that each security is linked to a particular candidate, and its price is the same as the predicted percentage of the vote that the candidate will win, according to the markets' traders.

Participants in the IEM trade use their own money and can set up accounts with $5 to $500. In general, IEM results are quite accurate and compare favorably with other ways of predicting the winners of political contests. Across twelve national elections in five countries, for example, the average margin of error of the last large-scale voter polls taken before the election was 1.93 percent. The average margin of error of the final IEM markets prices was 1.49 percent.[17]

The Hollywood Stock Exchange, a Web-based prediction market devoted to movies that does not use real money, provides another example of crowd wisdom. Its traders usually arrive at a highly accurate prediction concerning how much money a Hollywood movie will make during its opening weekend.[18] This accuracy is particularly impressive because movie revenues have proved extremely difficult to forecast using other means; as University of California, Irvine, Professor Arthur de Vany summarized, "My research . . . shows (and every movie fan knows) that motion picture revenues are not forecastable; the forecast error is infinite."[19] Screenwriter William Goldman famously distilled this conclusion to "nobody knows anything." The Hollywood

Stock Exchange and other prediction markets seem to show, in contrast, that many people can know many things.

In *The Wisdom of Crowds*, Surowiecki wrote that ". . . the most mystifying thing about [prediction] markets is how little interest corporate America has shown in them. Corporate strategy is all about collecting information from many different sources, evaluating the probabilities of potential outcomes, and making decisions in the face of an uncertain future. These are tasks for which [prediction] markets are tailor-made. Yet companies have remained, for the most part, indifferent to this source of potentially excellent information, and have been surprisingly unwilling to improve their decision making by tapping into the collective wisdom of their employees."[20]

Cowgill shared Surowiecki's puzzlement as he read his book, and came to believe that prediction markets were a natural technology for Google. The company's stated mission, after all, was "to organize the world's information and make it universally accessible and useful." Cowgill became intrigued by the idea of starting a prediction market at Google. He knew he'd need colleagues, particularly those with programming expertise, to help build one.[21]

Ilya Kirnos was exactly the kind of colleague Cowgill was looking for. He had programming expertise, and he shared Cowgill's interest in giving people a forum in which to make predictions. For Kirnos this interest sprang less from an interest in political elections and market mechanisms than from job frustrations he'd experienced. He had joined the advertising systems group at Google in 2004 after working at Oracle. Earlier in his career he had participated in a project that he and many other engineers knew would not succeed, but that continued to receive support and funding.

Kirnos wondered why it had been so hard to spread the word that this effort was doomed to fail, and he wanted to use technology at least to document the fact that he had accurately predicted its fate. Kirnos built a simple application called "itoldyouso" that allowed people to offer and accept nonmonetary bets and keep track of them over time. Employees could use it, for example, to essentially say to their colleagues, "I'll bet you this project won't be finished on time; any takers?" When they won a bet, the system helped them say, "I told you so!"[22]

Cowgill and Kirnos, however, did not know each other. Although they were employed by the same company, they worked in very dissimilar functions and would normally have little opportunity to meet and discover their common interests. Moreover, building prediction markets was not part of either of their job descriptions. How could they ever find each other, productively combine their talents, and create a technology to harness collective intelligence? And if a prediction market were ever built within Google, would it work as well as the IEM and Hollywood Stock Exchange did? Or would there be too few traders and trades to let markets work their magic and make accurate predictions?

Poor Tools

Each of the case studies just described is about collaborative work, and IT has a long history of activity in this area. The first conference on computer-supported collaborative work (CSCW), for example, was held in 1984, and over the years software vendors have offered many products intended to support interdependent teams and groups.

Yet none of the decision makers in the case studies presented here considered using groupware or knowledge management

(KM) software, the two classic applications of corporate CSCW. "Groupware" is a catch-all label for software such as Lotus Notes, which allows members of work teams to message each other, share documents and schedules, and build customized applications. Just as its name implies, groupware aims to help people with a common purpose work together by giving them access to a shared pool of information and communication tools. After the first version of Notes was released in 1989, groupware became quite widespread. Many organizations used the messaging and calendaring functionality of their groupware heavily but found the software less well suited to finding and sharing information and knowledge. One review of groupware research concluded that "In practice, Lotus Notes . . . is merely a glorified e-mail program."[23]

After groupware, KM systems were the second main group-level technology deployed widely in the 1980s and 1990s. KM systems essentially consisted of two components: a database designed to capture human knowledge about a particular topic—the best ways to sell mobile phones, the problems that cropped up among photocopiers at customer sites and how to fix them, tax law changes and how to interpret them—and a front-end application used by people to populate this database. KM systems were intended to receive "brain dumps" from people over time—their experiences, expertise, learnings, insights, and other types of knowledge. In most cases, though, they fell far short of this goal. As knowledge and technology researcher Tom Davenport of Babson College concluded, "The dream . . . that knowledge itself—typically unstructured, textual knowledge—could easily be captured, shared, and applied to knowledge work . . . [has not] been fully realized . . . it's taken much longer than anyone anticipated."[24]

Davenport's downbeat conclusion was amply supported by a survey he conducted in 2005 to determine what communications technologies people actually used in their work. As the results showed (see figure 2-1), classic groupware and KM systems didn't even make the list (although to be fair, by 2005 most groupware contained both e-mail and instant messaging functionality).

So by the middle of this century's first decade, corporate managers had reason to be skeptical that IT could *ever* be used effectively to knit together groups of people, letting them both create and share knowledge as a community. The technologies popular at that time for *producing* information (according to Davenport's research)—e-mail and instant messaging (IM)—were used for one-to-one or one-to-many communications; they

FIGURE 2-1

Percentage of knowledge workers using each medium weekly

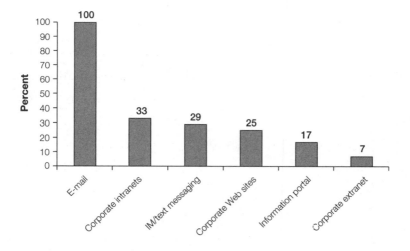

Source: Thomas H. Davenport, *Thinking for a Living: How to Get Better Performance and Results from Knowledge Workers* (Boston: Harvard Business School Press, 2005).

aided personal productivity but didn't enhance group functionality. On the other hand, the most popular technologies for
consuming information, intranets and public Web sites, were created, updated, and maintained by only a few people, not by all
members of a workgroup.

To understand why groupware, KM, and other "classic"
CSCW applications are so unpopular and why they were not se-
riously considered in any of the case studies described above,
we need to go back in time a short way and focus our attention
not on organizations, but instead on the World Wide Web. In
the early and middle years of the millennium's first decade a set
of new tools and new communities began to appear on the
Web. As we'll see, they are quite powerful. They overcome the
limitations of earlier tools for CSCW and assist greatly in re-
solving the problems in each of this chapter's case studies.

3

Web 2.0 and the Emergence of Emergence

A History, Explanation, and Definition

of Enterprise 2.0

B efore presenting the resolution of each of the cases discussed in chapter 2, we first need to understand a few recent technological developments. These occurred on the public Internet, where they gave rise to the phenomenon of Web 2.0. Web 2.0 is not mere "hype," nor is it of interest only to e-tailers and other Internet companies. Rather, it is extremely relevant to all organizations that want to bring people together into communities that generate useful information and knowledge and solve problems effectively. In other words, the new tools of Web 2.0 are very much applicable to VistaPrint, Serena, the U.S. intelligence community, and Google—and to your organization as well.

This chapter explains what the new tools are and why they truly are something new under the sun. It also describes some of the powerful new resources and communities, like Wikipedia and Delicious, that have sprung up around them on the Internet. Finally, it defines what I have termed *Enterprise 2.0*, the phenomenon that occurs when organizations adopt the tools and approaches of Web 2.0. In chapter 4 we'll return to the case studies to see four distinct examples of Enterprise 2.0 in action.

You don't need to be a technology professional, or even a technophile or gadget lover, to understand this chapter, or to profit from Enterprise 2.0. You simply need to understand three trends and appreciate how they combine to yield a new and improved set of digital tools.

A New Version of the Web?

In September 2005 the technology writer and publisher Tim O'Reilly posted the following entry, titled "What Is Web 2.0?" on his company's Web site:[1]

> The concept of "Web 2.0" began with a conference brainstorming session between O'Reilly and MediaLive International. Dale Dougherty, web pioneer and O'Reilly VP, noted that far from having "crashed," the web was more important than ever, with exciting new applications and sites popping up with surprising regularity. What's more, the companies that had survived the collapse seemed to have some things in common. Could it be that the dotcom collapse marked some kind of turning point for the web, such that a call to action such as "Web 2.0" might make sense? We agreed that it did . . .

O'Reilly and his colleagues examined companies, organizations, and sites that represented Web 2.0. These included the following:

- The collaboratively produced encyclopedia Wikipedia

- Social networking sites Facebook and MySpace

- Web-bookmarking resource Delicious[2]

- Media-sharing sites YouTube (for videos) and Flickr (for photos)

- Blogging utilities such as Blogger and Typepad and the blog-tracking site Technorati

- Web search engine Google

- Location-based classified ad site craigslist

Most of these had appeared quite recently, a fact that lent support to the notion that there was in fact a new version of the Web. Further support for this idea came from the enormous popularity of many of these resources. According to the Alexa ranking service, by August 2008 six of the ten most popular sites in the world—Google, YouTube, Facebook, MySpace, Wikipedia, and Blogger—were part of the new Web described by O'Reilly. People were voting with their feet (or, to be more precise, their mouse clicks), and were migrating with startling speed away from Web 1.0 stalwarts to the Web 2.0 start-ups.

In a December 2006 post to his blog, O'Reilly offered a short definition: *"Web 2.0 is the business revolution in the computer industry caused by the move to the Internet as platform, and an attempt to understand the rules for success on that new platform. Chief among those rules is this: Build applications that harness network effects to get better the more people use them.*"3 O'Reilly's definition was very helpful. It articulated and crystallized important developments on the Internet and throughout the high-tech sector. But what about companies *outside* the computer industry? Did the new sites and communities, and the principles that underlie them, herald any important business changes for them? And what about executives, managers, and front-line employees who weren't involved in building applications? What, if anything, did the new collaboration technologies and approaches mean for them? In other words, could VistaPrint, Serena, Google, and the U.S. intelligence community learn anything from Wikipedia, Blogger, and YouTube? What could "normal" organizations take away from the strange and wonderful new communities of Web 2.0?

To answer these questions, it's necessary first to understand what changed—how the IT "toolkit" available for collaboration and interaction became significantly larger and better in the first few years of the millennium than it was during the era of groupware and knowledge management (KM) systems.

O'Reilly's definition highlights *network effects*: the fact that some resources, like telephone networks and person-to-person auction Web sites, become more valuable to each member as they attract more and more members. Network effects are clearly fundamental, but nothing new; they were understood and deeply appreciated in many industries both before and after the arrival of the Internet. And network effects apply to many, if not most, communication and collaboration technologies, including e-mail, instant messaging (IM), groupware, and KM.

Three Trends Yield Better Tools

Network effects were a necessary but not sufficient condition in the transition from Web 1.0 to Web 2.0. To understand this transition more fully, and to appreciate what it means for all companies hoping to use technology in pursuit of business goals, we'll need to become familiar with three recent trends. On the Internet the convergence of these three trends has led to Web 2.0. Enterprise 2.0 describes the same convergence on corporate intranets and extranets. I'll give a tighter definition of Enterprise 2.0 after describing its underlying trends.

1. Free and Easy Platforms for Communication and Interaction

Some popular collaboration technologies—including e-mail, mobile phone texting, and some types of IM—are what I call *channels*. They essentially keep communications private. People beyond the sender and receiver(s) can't view the contents of information sent over channels and usually don't even know that communication has taken place. Information sent via channels isn't widely visible, consultable, or searchable. Because no record exists of who sent what to whom, channels leave no trace of collaboration patterns.

At times, of course, this is exactly what people want. Communications that are meant to be private should indeed take place via channels. Many other communications and collaborations, however, do not need to be private and may in fact benefit from greater visibility. If a knowledge worker finds herself sending the same e-mail over and over again in response to questions from colleagues, for example, she may well want the ability to display the information somewhere public and point people to it (or, better yet, let them find it on their own). Team members may want to discuss the problems they're working on publicly, so that others can help out if they have relevant knowledge. Channel technologies, unfortunately, aren't much help in either of these scenarios.

The alternative to a channel is what I call a *platform*. Platforms are simply collections of digital content where contributions are globally visible (everyone with access to the platform can see them) and persistent (they stick around, and so can be consulted and searched for). Access to platforms can be restricted—for example, to only members of an R&D lab or a team working on a particular deal—so that sensitive content isn't visible too widely, but the main goal of a platform technology is to make content widely and permanently available to its members.

Digital platforms are not rare; every Web site, whether on an intranet, extranet, or the Internet, is a platform. They're not new, either; companies and people have been building Web sites since the mid-1990s. To see what kinds of platforms *are* new in the era of Web 2.0, recall the journalist A. J. Liebling's mordant observation that "freedom of the press is limited to those who own one." In the mid-1990s, the World Wide Web put a multimedia printing press *and* a global distribution network in the hands of everyone with a little bandwidth, a bit of money (for site-hosting fees), and moderate technical expertise (for coding HTML pages and uploading them to servers). Millions of people and companies took advantage of this opportunity. Hundreds of millions of people did not, however, even though they had Internet access.

Lots of these people, of course, had nothing to say or no desire to take advantage of the printing press offered by the Web.

Many others, however, were daunted by the combination of time, expense, and technical skill required to set up and maintain their own Web site. I purchased the domain name mcafee.org many years ago, before the antivirus software company McAfee, Inc. (no relation, sadly) thought to pick it up, but I never did anything with it. My few attempts at coding HTML and maintaining a decent page, let alone a decent site, taught me that it was a *lot* of work, and I had plenty of other things to do.

Then blogs appeared, vastly reducing the amount of work required to publish on the Web. The term *weblog*, which was first used in 1997, came to refer to an individual's frequently updated Web site. In 1999 the shortened form *blog* first appeared as a noun and a verb. By the start of the millennium, software tools were available that let people initiate and update blogs without having to transfer files to servers manually or learn HTML. With these tools, people simply used their Internet browser to enter text, links to other Web sites, and the other elements of a standard blog.

Blogs let people add online content with no hassle and no knowledge of low-level technical details. They're an example of what I call *free and easy platforms*. In this description, *free* really does mean free of charge. Several advanced blogging platforms are available on the Web at no cost, so anyone with access to a connected computer can start contributing to the Internet's global pool of information.

Free and easy platforms now exist on the Web for all types of media, including images, videos, sound, and text. And many of the currently popular Web 2.0 platforms like Facebook, MySpace, and Blogger allow their users to combine many types of media—all without having to pay anything or acquire skills beyond the ability to point, click, drag, drop, and type.

As I'm writing this, one of the most intriguing new free and easy platforms on the Web takes communications that have historically flowed through channels and migrates them to a platform. Twitter is a utility that lets people broadcast short messages—no more than 140 characters—to anyone and everyone who may be interested in reading them. These messages can be sent from a computer, mobile phone, PDA, and so on. Users tell Twitter which people they're interested in "following," and Twitter collects all messages from these people (and only these people) and presents them to the user in a chronological list. This list can be viewed on the same range of devices from which messages are sent. Users can reply to one another's messages, but unless specifically requested otherwise, these replies are *public*; they become part of the Twitter platform rather than flowing through a private channel.

Twitter members use the utility to give updates on their location, plans, status, current work, thoughts and impressions, and many other aspects of their personal and professional lives. With Twitter they don't have to guess in advance who might be interested in these updates, then use a channel technology to transmit them. Instead, they simply post their updates to a platform, letting others consume them at will. And if these updates spark a conversation or other type of follow-up, this too can take place on the public platform. It remains to be seen how successful or long-lived Twitter itself will be, but its current popularity indicates that there was pent-up demand for interaction and communication using platforms rather than channels.

Even though free and easy platforms are now widespread, many people still believe that it's difficult to contribute online content. Those of us who started using computers before the birth of the Web, or even in the Web 1.0 era, often carry around the assumption that only technophiles (or, to use a less polite term, nerds) have the skills required to add material to an online platform.

It's surprising how durable this assumption can be. In 2006 I was teaching an executive education program for senior executives, owners, and presidents of companies. I assigned a case I had written about the internal use of blogs at a bank and gave out one additional bit of homework: I pointed the participants to Blogger and told them to start their own blogs and report the blogs' Internet addresses to me. What they reported instead was that they had no intention of completing the assignment. They told me how busy they were and said they had neither time nor inclination to mess around with blogs (whatever those were). Out of two classes with fifty to sixty participants each, I received fewer than fifteen blog addresses in all.

Trying to turn lemons into lemonade in class, I asked some of the people who had actually completed the task to describe the experience of starting a blog. They all shrugged and said it was no big deal, took about five minutes total, didn't require any skills, and so on. I then asked all the participants why they thought I would give busy executives such an easy assignment. In both classes one smart student piped up, "To show us exactly how easy it was." At that point, class discussion became interesting.

2. A Lack of Imposed Structure

As the entrepreneurs and technologists of Web 2.0 were building the new free and easy platforms, they were also rethinking their own roles and making a fundamental shift. Instead of imposing their own ideas about how content and work on the platforms should be structured, they started working hard to *avoid* such imposed structure. In this context *structure* means a few specific things:

- *Workflows:* The steps that need to be taken to accomplish a piece of work. A workflow is the flowchart of a business process specifying tasks, sequences, decision points, possible branches, and so on.

- *Decision rights:* Who has the authority, permission, power, or ability to do various things. For example, the decision right over equipment purchases up to $1,000 may be given to an entry-level engineer in an R&D lab, while the decision right for more expensive purchases rests with the lab manager.

- *Interdependencies:* Who will work together and what their relationship will be. Interdependencies are closely tied to both workflows and decision rights. A *workflow* defines which parties will be interdependent within a business process, while the allocation of *decision rights* determines whether these parties will be "above" or "below" each other.

- *Information:* What data will be included, how it will be formatted and displayed, how data elements will relate to one another, what kinds of error checking will take place, what will constitute "good" or "complete" information, and so on.

Throughout the history of corporate computing, the norm has been to use technology to *impose* these work structures—to define workflows, interdependencies, decision rights allocations, and/or information needs—in advance and then use software to put them in place. ERP (enterprise resource planning), CRM (customer relationship management), SCM (supply chain management), procurement, and other types of "enterprise systems" enjoyed explosive growth starting in the mid-1990s. These applications differed in many respects, but they shared one fundamental similarity: they were used to define, then deploy, business processes that cut across several organizational groups, thus helping to ensure that the processes would be executed the same way every time in every location. The applications did so by imposing all the elements of work structure listed above.

The belief that technologies supporting collaborative work should impose work structures appears, in fact, to be an almost unquestioned assumption. Technology developers and corporate managers seem to have until quite recently shared the belief that good outcomes in group-level work come from tightly structured processes. This belief was reflected in the design of both groupware and KM systems. A review of groupware use by Paul Dourish of the University of California, Irvine, highlighted that fact that while the software was originally intended to facilitate "work as an improvised, moment-by-moment accomplishment," it actually wound up being used to support workflows. According to Dourish, software containing "predefined formal descriptions of working processes" has constituted "perhaps the most successful form of groupware technology in current use."[4] In other words, a genre of technology intended to support *unstructured* work has enjoyed its greatest success as a tool for *imposing work structures*. KM applications did not typically specify interdependencies between people or workflows, but they did tightly predefine the structure of the information to be included within the knowledge database, giving only certain people and groups the right to add to it.

It's easy to understand where this faith in structure origi-
nates. It's at least as old as the theories of the pioneering industrial engineer Frederick Winslow Taylor, who at the beginning
of the twentieth century advocated studying work to determine
the "one best way" of accomplishing it and then making sure
that all workers followed the new standard. Later in the century,
the quality revolution led by W. Edwards Deming, Joseph
Juran, and others stressed that the best way to ensure consistently satisfactory outcomes was *not* to focus on the outcomes
themselves, but rather to control the process used to create
them. This could mean, for example, taking away a worker's
right to adjust his machine after it generated a single bad part
and giving this right instead to an engineer who will use the
techniques of statistical process control to determine if the machine had truly drifted out of specification. These techniques
and the philosophy underlying them soon spread from the manufacturing sector to many other industries, to the point where
standardized, tightly defined processes became an almost universal goal.

The work design philosophy of good outcomes via imposed
structure and tight control is clearly appropriate in many circumstances, but is it *always* appropriate? Are there circumstances or contexts in which it's better *not* to try to impose
control? Can high-quality outcomes result from an undefined,
nonstandardized, uncontrolled process?

The early history of Wikipedia provides a fascinating case
study of these issues. Wikipedia is now famous as the online encyclopedia that anyone can edit. The Wikipedia community
and the wiki technology that supports it, in other words, make
virtually no attempt to impose any of the elements of work
structure listed above: workflows and interdependencies are not

specified in advance, nor is the information that must be contained in each article. Neither is there much in the way of explicit allocation of important decision rights. The Wikipedia community does have administrators, bureaucrats, and stewards who are appointed or elected to their positions, but these groups are not supposed to have any greater say in creating or modifying articles than would a newly arrived Wikipedian. As cofounder Jimmy Wales wrote in a 2003 e-mail, "I just wanted to say that becoming [an administrator] is *not a big deal*. . . I want to dispel the aura of "authority" around the position. It's merely a technical matter that the powers given to [administrators] are not given out to everyone."[5]

Wikipedia's egalitarianism and lack of imposed structure are so deeply entrenched and widely accepted now that it's hard to believe that the community ever operated under a different set of ground rules. Yet it did. Founders Wales and Larry Sanger always had the goal of creating a high-quality encyclopedia that would be available free worldwide via the Internet. But they initially took the standard approach to ensuring high-quality results: they tightly structured the content-creation process. The first organization they created to build a Web-based encyclopedia was called Nupedia.

As its Wikipedia entry states, ". . . Nupedia was characterized by an extensive peer review process designed to make its articles of a quality comparable to that of professional encyclopedias." Sanger, Wales, and an advisory board consisting of PhDs in a variety of fields set up the following seven-stage content-creation process for Nupedia:

1. *Article assignment:* Once an article topic had been proposed by a user, they identified the area editor (e.g., in

philosophy, chemistry, sociology) and decided whether or not that user was qualified to write such an article. If the user was not qualified, the area editor attempted to find someone else with the right qualifications to write the article.

2. *Lead reviewer selection:* Following article assignment, the editor found a reviewer in the field, an expert in that domain, to read and anonymously critique the article.

3. *Lead review:* The lead review process was blind and confidential. The author, reviewer, and editor corresponded on a private Web site to determine whether or not the article met Nupedia's standards for inclusion.

4. *Open review:* Once an article passed lead review, it was then "opened" up to the general public for review. An article had to be approved by the section editor, lead reviewer, and at least one category peer reviewer before it was deemed suitable for publication.

5. *Lead copyediting:* Once an article had passed open review, an e-mail was sent to Nupedia's list of copyeditors asking participants to sign up to copyedit the article. The author selected two volunteer editors and worked with them to get the article ready for the next stage.

6. *Open copyediting:* After lead copyrighting was finished, an open copyediting period, lasting at least a week, was set aside so that members of the general public could make changes. Final edits were approved by the two lead copyeditors.

7. *Final approval and markup:* After the category editor and
   two lead copyeditors had given their final approval, the
   article was posted on Nupedia. At the end of this
   process the article's original author was eligible for a
   free Nupedia T-shirt or coffee cup.[6]

Not everyone could participate in Nupedia; a policy document stated, "We wish editors to be true experts in their fields
and (with few exceptions) possess PhDs."[7]

After eighteen months of operation and $250,000 in expen-
ditures, the Nupedia site contained only twelve articles.[8]

In the fall of 2000, concerned by the lack of positive momentum in Nupedia, Wales and Sanger started to investigate alternative models for content production. On January 2, 2001,
Ben Kovitz had lunch with his friend Sanger and told him
about *wikis*, Ward Cunningham's technology to enhance collaboration among software developers.

Cunningham had found it difficult to share his innovations
and knowledge concerning software development techniques
with his colleagues. In 1995 he addressed this problem by creating Web pages that could be not only read but also edited by
any reader. He called his creation *WikiWikiWeb*, which was later
shortened to *wiki*.

Users can add, delete, or edit any part of a wiki. A wiki is
typically supported by a database that keeps track of all
changes, allowing users to compare changes and also revert to
any previous version. With a wiki, all contributions are stored
permanently and all actions are visible and reversible.

Sanger thought that a wiki might help solve the problems
facing Nupedia. On the evening following his lunch with Kovitz
he let Wales know about his new discovery and recommended

that they experiment with a "wikified" Nupedia. Most of the members of the advisory board were not interested in a free-for-all encyclopedia construction project, but Wales and Sanger decided to proceed with the experiment.

On January 15, 2001, Wales and Sanger set up a separate Web site—www.wikipedia.com—supported by wiki technology. Sanger sent a note to the Nupedia volunteers list encouraging its members to check out this new attempt: "Humor me. Go there and add a little article. It will take all of five or ten minutes."[9]

At the end of January there were 617 articles on Wikipedia. March saw 2,221 articles on the new platform, July 7,243, and December approximately 19,000. On September 26, 2003, Nupedia was formally shut down. It had 24 completed articles.

As of June 2008, Wikipedia was by far the largest reference work in the world, with more than 2.4 million articles in English, more than 500,000 each in German, Polish, and French, and more than 250,000 in each of six other languages. Clearly, the founders' shift in philosophy away from imposed work structures and toward the use of wiki technology supporting the new approach of freeform, egalitarian collaboration unleashed a huge amount of energy and enthusiasm. But did it lead to the creation of high-quality encyclopedia entries, or to the proliferation of junk? We'll take up that question shortly.

Yahoo!'s purchase in late 2005 of the Web-based bookmarking site Delicious provides another example of the same broad shift in philosophy away from imposed structure, in this case the structure of the millions of pages that make up the Web. Early in its history Yahoo!'s founders said that it stood for "Yet Another Hierarchical Officious Oracle," poking fun at themselves but also revealing their vision for the company. Yahoo! attempted to organize the Web's content into a hierarchical structure, placing individual sites into predefined categories like Health, Arts, and Computers and then creating subcategories within them. Below are a couple of pictures of Yahoo!'s home page showing how this categorization evolved over time (see figure 3-1).

The company employed taxonomists to create and update this structure. Taxonomy is the science of classifying things, usually hierarchically. Carl Linnaeus's classification of living things—by kingdom, phylum, class, order, family, genus, and species—is perhaps the best-known example. Taxonomies are developed by experts and then rolled out to users to help them make sense of the world and relate things to one another.

I used to use Yahoo!'s taxonomy of the Web a lot. I stopped when I sensed that the Web was becoming too big and growing

FIGURE 3-1

December 1998 Yahoo! homepage showing its web categorization

Source: http://web.archive.org/web/*/http://yahoo.com.

too fast; the professional taxonomists couldn't keep up. As figures 3-2 and 3-3 show, Yahoo!'s taxonomy also became less important to the company itself over time. It occupied successively less and less of the home page, the company's prime Web real estate, and disappeared from it altogether in August 2006.

I didn't pay much more attention to Web categorization schemes until I started hearing about Delicious. Delicious is a Web site that lets members store all their bookmarks on the Web itself so that they're accessible from anywhere. More importantly, it allows members to add *tags* to those sites—simple, one-word

FIGURE 3-2

December 2004 Yahoo! homepage showing its Web categorization near the bottom of the page

Source: http://web.archive.org/web/*/http://yahoo.com.

FIGURE 3-3

August 2006 Yahoo! homepage*

Source: http://web.archive.org/web/*/http://yahoo.com.

* The company's taxonomy of the Web no longer appears.

descriptions that serve as reminders of what the page is about and also enable users to group sites together.

My Delicious tags include "blogs," "web2.0," and "business." I generated these tags on my own, instead of selecting them from any predefined list. When choosing a tag, I was able to enter any string of letters, numbers, and symbols that made sense to me. I couldn't do anything remotely like this with Yahoo!, where I could only passively accept the company's taxonomy but had no real ability to extend or modify it. Delicious does no error checking or second-guessing; it "allowed" both "enterprise2.0" and "enterprise2.0,". In sharp contrast to the original Yahoo! taxonomy, Delicious imposes no structure on the Web's content. Instead, it lets me and all other users create whatever categorizations are useful for ourselves.

A broad concern about this approach, though, is that it leads to messiness. If no one is telling me and all the other

Delicious users what tags are acceptable—if we're all able to enter as many different strings of letters and numbers as we like—won't it be impossible for Delicious itself ever to add up to anything? Won't it become just a huge sprawling collection of individuals' idiosyncratic bookmarks and tags, with little commonality or overlap? In short, if some entity (like Yahoo!) doesn't predefine a structure (like its Web categorization) and then take responsibility for placing things within that structure, isn't chaos the inevitable result? To see why this is *not* always the case, and to understand the third trend underlying Web 2.0 and Enterprise 2.0, it will be helpful to review a bit of history.

Figure 3-4 shows my Delicious tags at one point in time. The number shows how many times I've used that tag.[10]

FIGURE 3-4

Delicious tags at one point in time

```
  ▽ tags
  1  2005
  2  APMblog
  1  BBC
  3  blogs
  1  business
  1  cases
  1  concentration
  1  del.icio.us
  1  delicious
  1  DrKW
  3  enterprise2.0
  2  enterprise2.0,
  9  HBS
  1  humor
  1  interoperability
  1  news
  1  newspapers
  1  nyc
  1  OPM
  1  personal
  1  political
  1  politics
  3  SOA
```

3. Mechanisms to Let Structure Emerge

Several years ago the mathematician and writer John Allen Paulos gave voice to a widespread concern about the Web's growth with the observation, "The Internet is the world's largest library. It's just that all the books are on the floor." He meant that there was no equivalent of a card catalog for the Web's content. People who put up Web sites were under no obligation to categorize their contents accurately, and there was nothing like the Dewey Decimal or Library of Congress system to classify what a site was about. Yahoo! tried to do this on its own by employing many people to look at Web sites and place them within the company's hierarchy of online content. This approach worked for a time, but eventually the Web grew too fast for Yahoo! to keep up.

Web 1.0 search engines developed by Lycos, Alta Vista, Infoseek, Excite, HotBot, and others provided an alternative to Yahoo!'s hierarchy. They worked by automatically visiting as many sites as possible, a process known as "Web crawling," and analyzing their content, primarily their text, to determine what they were about. Lycos, Alta Vista, and their early competitors looked at each page in isolation, relying either on its key words and how often they appeared, on the page's description of itself—typically contained in its "metadata," a special section of the page's HTML code invisible to human viewers—or on some combination of these and other factors.

There were two serious problems with this approach to searches. First, if several Web sites existed on the same topic, it was difficult to determine which was the best. If, for example, five pages were devoted to the Boston Red Sox, which should the search engine rank highest—the one that used the team's name most often? Second, it relied on the accuracy of the Web sites' and pages' own descriptions. And since search results drive Web traffic and Web traffic generates advertising revenue and e-commerce sales, Web site owners had strong incentives to misrepresent what their sites and pages were about. They could do this either by lying in their pages' metadata or by adding key terms like *Boston Red Sox* thousands of times in the Web's equivalent of invisible ink. These two factors combined to make Web searching an intensely frustrating experience for many people, a feeling captured in Paulos's quote. In December 1998 the online magazine *Salon.com* chronicled the results of a search for "President Clinton": "Infoseek does a decent job returning the Oval Office site at the top of the list, but Excite sends you to an impeachment poll on Tripod and the Paula Jones Legal Defense Fund—the president's page doesn't even make it into the first 10 results. Hotbot's top result is a site called Tempting Teens—" 'All the Kinky Things that make our Government what it is.' "[11]

The *Salon.com* article, written by Scott Rosenberg, identified a newly available engine that did a better job of returning relevant results. It was called Google, and it took a very different approach to search. Google relied on *other* sites to determine how good a given site was, and therefore how prominently it should be featured in search results. Google's founders, Larry Page and Sergey Brin, were PhD students at Stanford and were inspired in part by the standard method for judging academic papers: a good academic paper is one that's referenced or cited by many other papers, and "citation indexes" have long been used by scholars.

Page and Brin realized that the authors of Web pages cite one another just the way the authors of scholarly papers do. But on the Web, citations take the form of links from one page to another. The two students developed an algorithm that ranked pages based on how many other pages linked to them, giving more weight to pages that were themselves heavily linked to. It is this algorithm, which came to be known as PageRank, that lies at the heart of the Google search engine.

Google was the first search engine to view the Web as a community rather than a collection of individual sites, to realize that members of this community referenced one another heavily via hyperlinks (just as members of a scientific community do via citations), and to use these links to determine ranking within the community. Search engines stand or fall based on how good their rankings are, and from its inception Google's appeared to be very good indeed. In his *Salon.com* article, Rosenberg wrote, "Since discovering Google a few weeks ago, I've been so impressed with its usefulness and accuracy that I've made it my first search stop."

Since December 1998 many, many people have joined him. In June 2006 the Oxford English Dictionary included the verb "to Google," meaning, "To use the Google search engine to find information on the Internet . . . To search for information about (a person or thing) using the Google search engine."[12]

Page and Brin realized that Paulos's image of the Web as a mountain of valuable but unstructured content was vivid but wrong. Web content is not unstructured; it is in fact highly structured as a result of all the links from one page to another. This structure can be exploited not just for navigation (hopping from page to page via links) but also for searching. Links provide so much structure, in fact, that the Web appears to us to be a very orderly place; thanks to Google, we can find what we want on it.

Ant colonies are similar to the Web in that they appear highly structured even though no central authority is in charge. Colonies have complex social structures and use sophisticated strategies to forage, defend themselves, and make war. This happens not because the queen ant sends out orders, but because each ant is programmed by its DNA to do certain things (carry an egg, fight an intruder, go to where food is) in response to local signals (usually chemical scents from other ants, eggs, intruders, food, and so on). As ants interact with one another and their environment, they send and receive signals, and these low-level activities yield high-level structure.

Complexity science uses the term *emergent* to describe systems such as ant colonies and the Web. *Emergence* is the appearance of global structure as the result of local interactions. It doesn't happen in most systems; what's necessary is a set of mechanisms to do critical things such as connecting the system's elements and providing feedback among them.

The Web's emergent nature doesn't stem from the fact that it's a huge collection of digital documents; if the contents of the Library of Congress were digitized tomorrow and put online, they would not constitute an emergent system. The Web is emergent because it's the dynamic creation of countless people around the world interacting with one another via links as they create new content.

This is a key difference between the public Internet and most corporate intranets today. Whereas public Web sites are built by millions of people, most intranets are built and maintained by a small group. Emergence requires large numbers of actors and interactions, but intranets are produced by only a few people (even though they are passively consumed by many). In addition, most intranet pages aren't as heavily inter-linked as pages on the Internet.

Tagging, as implemented on Delicious and many other sites, is another way to let structure emerge over time. As discussed above, I and all the other Delicious users have complete freedom to define our own tags. It turns out, though, that we tend to use the same relatively small group of words as tags to describe Web pages that we've bookmarked. Delicious takes advantage of this fact in several ways. For example, the site includes "tag clouds," which are views of the most popular tags. Figure 3-5 shows a tag cloud for all Delicious users at one point in time; it's arranged alphabetically, with the size of the word indicating its relative popularity. Shaded tags are ones that I've used; this feature helps me understand where I fit into the universe of Delicious users. Clicking on any word brings up a list of the Web pages that have been tagged with that word, so that users can also see what other tags have been applied to that page, how many Delicious users have tagged the page, and the

FIGURE 3-5

The Delicious tag cloud at one point in time

ajax art audio blog blogs books business car community computer cool CSS culture daily design development diy download dvd education email entertainment finance firefox flash food forum free freeware fun funny game games google graphics hacking hacks hardware health history home howto humor inspiration internet ipod java javascript job jobs language linux mac marketing media microsoft mobile movies mozilla mp3 music network news online opensource personal photo photography photos php podcast politics programming radio recipes reference research reviews rss ruby science search security server shopping social software sports tech technology tips tools toread travel tutorial tutorials tv video web web2.0 webdesign webdev windows wizzrss work

(red tags are tags you share with everyone else)

Source: Delicious.

collection of pages and tags associated with each user (if they give permission for this data to be made public).

The information architect Thomas Vander Wal describes a tag cloud as a *folksonomy*, a categorization system developed over time by folks. A folksonomy is an alternative to a *taxonomy*, which is a categorization system developed at a single point in time by an authority. Taxonomies are not always inferior, and they haven't become irrelevant in the Internet era; the classification of living things into kingdoms, phyla, classes, orders, families, genuses, and species is a long-standing and very useful taxonomy. But the success of Delicious indicates that folksonomies offer advantages for categorizing multidimensional and fast-changing content.

Tagging, like linking, fulfills the standard criteria for emergence:

- It's conducted by many agents spread all over a digital platform like the Internet.

- These agents are acting independently and with great autonomy. I don't pick my tags from any predefined list; I make up whatever ones are useful to me.

- Agents are also acting in their own self-interest. My Delicious tags help *me* navigate my own bookmarks. The fact that they help reveal the Web's structure to everyone else is peripheral to me, but central to the value of Delicious for everyone else.

The high-level structure of the Delicious folksonomy, which changes over time and is visible in its cloud views, can't be predicted by observing low-level activities. My tags, in other words, won't tell you anything about what's going on across Delicious as a whole, just as watching a single ant won't tell you what the entire colony is up to. Complexity science uses the term *irreducible* to describe this sharp disconnect between low-level behaviors and high-level structure.

Like the PageRank algorithm, tags, folksonomies, and tag clouds of online content are relatively recent innovations. Delicious first appeared in 2003; the photo-sharing Web site Flickr, sometimes credited with showing the Web's first tag clouds, was launched in 2004. Tagging has since spread to other popular Web 2.0 sites like YouTube and Facebook.

All of these sites are examples of what I call *emergent social software platforms* (ESSPs). Let's break this definition down a bit. *Social software* enables people to rendezvous, connect, or collaborate through computer-mediated communication and to form online communities.[13] *Platforms*, as discussed above, are digital environments in which contributions and interactions are globally visible and persistent over time. *Emergent* means that the software is freeform and contains mechanisms like links and tags to let the patterns and structure inherent in people's interactions become visible over time. *Freeform* means that the software is most or all of the following:

- Optional

- Free of imposed structure such as workflow, interdependencies, and decision right allocations

- Egalitarian, or indifferent to credentials, titles, and other forms of "rank"

- Accepting of many types of data

ESSPs share a few technical features, which I summarize
with the acronym *SLATES* (*s*earch, *l*inks, *a*uthoring, *t*agging,
*e*xtensions, *s*ignals).

- *Search:* For any information platform to be valuable, its
  users must be able to find what they are looking for.
  Web page layouts and navigation aids can help with
  this, but users are increasingly bypassing these in favor
  of keyword searches. It might seem that orderly intranets maintained by a professional staff would be easier to search than the huge, dynamic, uncoordinated
  Internet, but a simple survey shows that this is evidently not the case.

  I start many of my speeches and presentations by asking people to raise their hands if it's easier for them to
  find what they want on their company's intranet than it
  is on the public Internet. Very few people have ever
  raised their hands.

- *Links:* As discussed above, links are the main reason
  that searching on the Internet (thanks to Google and
  similar search engines) is so much more satisfying than
  doing so on most intranets. Search technology like
  Google's works best when there's a dense link structure
  that changes over time and reflects the opinions of
  many people. This is the case on the Internet, but not
  on most of today's intranets, where links are made only
  by the relatively small internal Web development
  group. In order for this to change within companies,
  many people have to be given the ability to make links.
  The most straightforward way to accomplish this end is

to let the intranet be authored by a large group rather than a small one.

- *Authoring:* Blogs and Wikipedia have shown that many people have a desire to author, that is, write for a broad audience. As wiki inventor Ward Cunningham said, "I wanted to stroke that story-telling nature in all of us . . . I wanted people who wouldn't normally author to find it comfortable authoring, so that there stood a chance of us discovering the structure of what they had to say."[14] Cunningham's point is not that there are a lot of undiscovered Shakespeares out there, but rather that most people have *something* to contribute, whether it's knowledge, insight, experience, a fact, an edit, a link, and so on; authorship is a way to elicit these contributions. When authoring tools are used within a company, the intranet platform shifts from being the creation of a few to becoming the constantly updated, interlinked work of many.

- *Tags:* A survey from Forrester Research revealed that what experienced users wanted most from their companies' intranets, after better searching mechanisms, was better categorization of content.[15] Sites like Delicious and Flickr aggregate large amounts of content and then essentially outsource the work of categorization to their users by letting them attach tags. These sites don't try to impose an up-front categorization scheme; instead they let one emerge over time as a result of users' actions, which collectively create a folksonomy. In addition to building folksonomies, tags provide a way to keep track of the platforms knowledge workers visit,

making patterns and processes in knowledge work more
visible as a result.

- *Extensions:* Moderately "smart" computers take tagging
  one step further by automating some of the work of categorization and pattern matching. They use algorithms
  to say to users, "If you liked that, then by extension
  you'll like this." Amazon's system of recommendations
  was one early example of the use of extensions on the
  Web. The browser toolbar from stumbleupon.com is
  another. With it, users simply select a topic they're
  interested in and hit the "stumble" button. They're
  then taken to a Web site on that topic. If they like it,
  they click a "thumbs up" button on the toolbar; if not,
  they click a "thumbs down" button. They next stumble
  onto another site. Over time, StumbleUpon matches
  preferences to send users only to sites they'll like. It's
  surprising how quickly, and how well, this simple system works. It reasons by extension, homing in on user
  tastes with great speed.

- *Signals:* Even with powerful tools to search and categorize platform content, a user can still feel overwhelmed. New content is added so often that it can
  become a full-time job just to check for updates on all
  sites of interest. The final element of the SLATES
  infrastructure is technology to signal users when
  new content of interest appears. Signals can come as
  e-mail alerts, but these contribute to overloaded in-
  boxes and may be treated as spam. A relatively novel
  technology called RSS (which usually refers to "really

simple syndication") provides another solution. Authors such as bloggers use RSS to generate a short notice each time they add new content. The notice usually consists of a headline that is also a link back to the full content. Software for users called "aggregators" or "readers" periodically queries sites of interest for new notices, downloads them, puts them in order, and displays their headlines. With RSS, users no longer have to surf constantly to check for changes; instead, they simply consult their aggregators, click on headlines of interest, and are taken to the new content.

With this background, it's now possible to give a more precise definition of Enterprise 2.0:

> *Enterprise 2.0* is the use of emergent social software platforms by organizations in pursuit of their goals.

This definition does not apply just to the computer industry—it's applicable to any setting in which ESSPs are deployed. And it focuses not on the Internet and social trends, but rather on organizations such as companies and public-sector agencies. Enterprise 2.0, then, is about how organizations use the newly available ESSPs to do their work better. These ESSPs can include all appropriate participants—employees, suppliers, customers, prospective customers, and so on. In other words, Enterprise 2.0 is not just about intranets and does not take place solely behind the firewall; it encompasses extranets and public Web sites as well.

I want to make for the first time a point that will be re-
peated throughout this book: Enterprise 2.0 is *not* primarily a
technological phenomenon. The preceding discussion stressed
tools—ESSPs and their building blocks. The appearance of
these novel tools is a necessary but not sufficient condition for
allowing new modes of interaction, collaboration, and innovation, and for delivering the benefits that will be discussed later
in this book. To make full use of these tools, however, organizations will have to do much more than simply deploy ESSPs;
they'll also have to put in place environments that encourage
and allow people to use ESSPs widely, deeply, and productively. On the Web, Wikipedia provides one example of such
an environment, showing how it came about and how effective
it can be.

The example of Wikipedia illustrates that some of the mechanisms of emergence are organizational and managerial, rather
than purely technical. In other words, leaders can't simply
assume that healthy communities will self-organize and act in
a coherent and productive manner after Web 2.0 tools are deployed. Organizations are not ant colonies, and an examination
of Wikipedia's history reveals that much effort has gone into
defining the social ground rules of the community so that its
members interact with one another in largely positive ways.
These ground rules fall into two groups: informal norms, and
formal policies and guidelines.

Norms

Founder Jimmy Wales summarized Wikipedia's norms this
way: "Our community has an atmosphere of love and respect
for each other, a real passion for the work, a real interest in

getting it right. We make it fun and easy for good people to get involved."[16]

Early Wikipedians worked to create a cooperative and helpful culture. Most decisions are made by consensus among senior members of the community. Votes are often taken, but their results are not binding; they're intended to provide information on a matter, not settle it. Overly harsh or argumentative contributors are corrected by their peers and barred if they are found repeatedly ignoring counsel and violating norms.

The wiki technology itself helps reinforce this culture because any participant has the ability to edit or remove anyone else's contribution. As a result, the incentive to create graffiti and deface entries essentially vanishes, since negative contributions can be erased with just a few clicks. As Wales has put it, "The wiki model is different because it gives you an incentive when you're writing. If you write something that annoys other people, it's just going to be deleted. So if you want your writing to survive, you really have to strive to be cooperative and helpful."[17]

Policies and Guidelines

To complement and reinforce these norms, the Wikipedia community formulated a set of policies and guidelines for editing. These have been summarized as the "five pillars of Wikipedia":

> Wikipedia is an encyclopedia incorporating elements of general encyclopedias, specialized encyclopedias, and almanacs. All articles must follow our no original research policy and strive for accuracy; Wikipedia is not the place to

insert personal opinions, experiences, or arguments. Furthermore, Wikipedia is not an indiscriminate collection of information. Wikipedia is not a trivia collection, a soapbox, a vanity publisher, an experiment in anarchy or democracy, or a web directory. Nor is Wikipedia a dictionary, a newspaper, or a collection of source documents.

Wikipedia has a neutral point of view, which means we strive for articles that advocate no single point of view. Sometimes this requires representing multiple points of view; presenting each point of view accurately; providing context for any given point of view, so that readers understand whose view the point represents; and presenting no one point of view as "the truth" or "the best view." It means citing verifiable, authoritative sources whenever possible, especially on controversial topics. When a conflict arises as to which version is the most neutral, declare a cool-down period and tag the article as disputed; hammer out details on the talk page and follow dispute resolution.

Wikipedia is free content that anyone may edit. All text is available under the GNU Free Documentation License (GFDL) and may be distributed or linked accordingly. Recognize that articles can be changed by anyone and no individual controls any specific article; therefore, any writing you contribute can be mercilessly edited and redistributed at will by the community. Do not submit copyright infringements or works licensed in a way incompatible with the GFDL.

Wikipedia has a code of conduct: Respect your fellow Wikipedians even when you may not agree with them. Be civil. Avoid making personal attacks or sweeping generalizations. Stay cool when the editing gets hot; avoid edit wars by following the three-revert rule; remember that there are 1,495,425 articles on the English Wikipedia to work on and discuss. Act in good faith, never disrupt Wikipedia to illustrate a point, and assume good faith on the part of others. Be open and welcoming.

Wikipedia does not have firm rules besides the five general principles elucidated here. Be bold in editing, moving, and modifying articles, because the joy of editing is that although it should be aimed for, perfection isn't required. And don't worry about messing up. All prior versions of articles are kept, so there is no way that you can accidentally damage Wikipedia or irretrievably destroy content. But remember—whatever you write here will be preserved for posterity.[18]

None of these policies and guidelines was in place when Larry Sanger sent out his e-mail to the Nupedia community in January 2001 asking them to experiment with the new wiki technology. Instead, they emerged over time as it became clear that more structure was needed. And as the final pillar of Wikipedia indicates, members of the community are aware that its structure continues to be emergent and will never be written in stone. As I write this section in mid-2008, for example, an active debate continues about whether Wikipedia should have stricter or looser criteria for including new articles and keeping versus deleting existing ones. "Deletionists" and "inclusionists" disagree on this topic and continue to argue their positions within the community.

How well do these norms and policies work? In late 2005 the scientific journal *Nature* conducted a study comparing the accuracy of science entries in Wikipedia with that of the online version of *Encyclopedia Britannica*. Experts examined the same set of 42 science articles from each reference work and noted both major and minor errors. The study found that *Encyclopedia Britannica* had 123 errors, whereas Wikipedia had 162, for averages of 2.9 and 3.9 errors per article respectively. Each encyclopedia had four major errors.

Timo Hannay, publishing director of nature.com and a blogger on *Nature*'s Web site, noted:

> Going through the subject-by-subject results, I make the final score 22-10 in favour of Britannica, with 10 draws . . . If you believe that an encyclopedia should be judged by its weakest entries (in general I don't), or if you're the subject of an error or slur (thankfully I'm nowhere near famous enough), then the anecdotal outliers might be more important to you than averaged results. But most readers simply want to know whether a source can generally be relied upon. What these results say to me is that Wikipedia isn't bad in this regard—and that if it's really important to get your facts right then even Britannica isn't completely dependable . . . A key outstanding question is whether or not Wikipedia can ever surpass Britannica in quality. Since it evidently already does in some subjects, I think the answer is yes, but we will have to wait and

see. Frankly, I still can't get over the fact that it
works at all.[19]

The study's list of errors on Wikipedia was made widely
available on December 22, 2005. By January 25, 2006, all of
them had reportedly been corrected.[20] Something about this
new way of organizing and collaborating was clearly working.

4

New Approaches to
Old Problems

Hitting the Bull's-Eye with Enterprise 2.0

Chapter 3 showed that emergent social software platforms (ESSPs) come in many forms and can be used in a wide variety of ways. Because of this, it might seem that Enterprise 2.0 is such a diverse phenomenon that it can't be boiled down at all, and will mean something different for every organization. But this is not the case. Even though there are a great many tools available, and even though every deployment of them will be unique, there are deep similarities.

The Concept of Tie Strength

To reveal these similarities, this chapter uses the concept of "tie strength" between people. Some deployments of ESSPs are intended to support ties that are already strong, while others are aimed at ties that are weak, or even nonexistent. The case studies in chapter 2 provide examples of the four different levels of tie strength, which this chapter presents as rings in an "Enterprise 2.0 Bull's-Eye." Awareness of this bull's-eye helps leaders decide where they want to focus their organization's Enterprise 2.0 efforts.

When observers have chronicled the world of work, they have often focused on relatively small groups of close-knit colleagues. This was certainly true of the landmark Hawthorne studies conducted from 1927 to 1932 by Elton Mayo and his associates at Harvard Business School. This research, which gave rise to the term "Hawthorne effect," documented the output, interactions, and attitudes over time of a team of assembly workers in a factory outside Chicago. The Hawthorne studies were revolutionary not only for their findings but also for their long duration and level of detail, and they established a template for much later work.[1]

The tendency to focus on small groups of close colleagues extends to fictional depictions of the working world, from Herman Melville's 1853 novella *Bartleby, the Scrivener* to the British and then American television series *The Office*. All of this work builds on, and reinforces, the perception that the interesting aspects of work are the activities and interactions of close colleagues.

A landmark paper in sociology, written over thirty-five years ago, offers a very different perspective. In 1973 Mark Granovetter's "The Strength of Weak Ties" appeared in the *American Journal of Sociology*. SWT, as the paper came to be known, advanced a novel theory, which Granovetter himself summarized in a follow-up article written ten years later: "The argument asserts that our acquaintances (*weak ties*) are less likely to be socially involved with each other than are our close friends (*strong ties*). Thus the set of people made up of any individual and his or her acquaintances comprises a low-density network (one in which many of the possible relational lines are absent) whereas the set . . . consisting of the same individual and his or her *close* friends will be densely knit (many of the possible lines are present)."[2]

Granovetter also laid out the critical implications of this assertion:

> The overall social structural pictures suggested by this argument can be seen by considering the situation of some arbitrarily selected individual—call him Ego. Ego will have a collection of close friends, most of whom are in touch with one another—a densely knit clump of social structure. Moreover, Ego will have a collection of acquaintances, few of whom will know each other. Each of these acquaintances, however, is likely to have close friends in his own right and therefore to be enmeshed in a closely knit clump of social structure, but one different from Ego's. *The weak tie between Ego and his acquaintance, therefore, becomes not merely a trivial acquaintance tie but rather a crucial bridge between the two densely knit clumps of close friends . . . these clumps would not, in fact, be connected to one another at all were it not for the existence of weak ties* (emphasis added).[3]

A tidy summary of SWT's conclusion is that strong ties are unlikely to be bridges between networks, while weak ties are good bridges. Bridges help solve problems, gather information, and import unfamiliar ideas. They enable work to be accomplished more quickly and more effectively. The ideal network

for a knowledge worker probably consists of a core of strong ties
and a large periphery of weak ones.

SWT made a fundamental contribution to the discipline
(as of July 2008 it had been cited by others an astonishing
7,100+ times, according to Google Scholar) because it focused
attention on a previously ignored area, and because it articulated tight and testable hypotheses about why weak ties were so
valuable.

In SWT Granovetter didn't focus on work environments,
but later research explored whether his hypotheses and conclusions apply within companies. Morton Hansen, for example,
found that weak ties helped product development groups accomplish projects quickly. Hansen, Marie Louise Mors, and
Bjorn Lovas further showed that weak ties helped by reducing
information search costs. And Daniel Levin and Rob Cross
found that the benefits of weak ties were amplified if knowledge
seekers trusted that the information sources in question were
competent in their fields.[4]

This research revealed that Granovetter might well have
been talking about companies when he wrote that ". . . social
systems lacking in weak ties will be fragmented and incoherent.
New ideas will spread slowly, scientific endeavors will be handicapped, and subgroups separated by . . . geography or other
characteristics will have difficulty reaching a *modus vivendi*."[5]

By 2007, the executives at Serena Software (the second of
the case studies in chapter 2) were becoming worried that their
company was devolving into exactly this kind of dysfunctional
and inefficient social system. The company had grown largely
by acquisition, had many offices around the world, and had a
workforce consisting of 35 percent telecommuters—people who
rarely if ever came into an office. In these circumstances it could

be difficult for Serena employees to form even weak social ties with one another. Granovetter's work implies that the lack of such ties would impede more than Serena's ability to build a healthy corporate culture; it would also impede its employees' ability to accomplish important and novel work.

A later body of influential sociological research focused not on ties, but on their absence. Like SWT, Ronald Burt's 1992 book *Structural Holes* analyzed social networks in a novel way and became heavily referenced (with more than four thousand Google Scholar citations by July 2008). Burt defined a structural hole as "a separation between nonredundant contacts," which he in turn defined as contacts that don't "lead to the same people, and so provide the same information benefits."[6]

In Burt's formulation structural holes are sometimes filled by people, and sometimes not. When they are not, information can't flow from one human network to the other. Ties span holes, and weak ties can be particularly valuable in this regard, but there is no guarantee that all structural holes, even the most important ones, will be filled. Burt's book emphasized that structural holes can be valuable to an individual if she can establish contacts that span them. When she accomplishes this task, she provides information benefits to both of the previously isolated networks and so increases her "social capital."

Unspanned structural holes may provide opportunities and be valuable from an individual's perspective, but from an enterprise perspective they are nothing but bad news. Because they prevent information from flowing, unspanned holes lead to the fragmented and handicapped social system described by Granovetter. As the federal commissions on the 9/11 attacks and the intelligence failures with regard to Iraqi weapons of mass destruction made clear, U.S. intelligence agencies were just such a system before 9/11, and even afterward. Many reports and news stories referred to the agencies' failure to "connect the dots" of available intelligence about the threats facing the country, unconsciously using precisely the imagery of social network analysis. In this case the dots were both pieces of information *and* the intelligence analysts who held this information. When these analysts were members of networks whose structural holes were *not* spanned, vital information did not flow as it needed to. In the language of network sociologists, the U.S. intelligence community was a "non-dense" network, that is, one in which few of the potential ties among members had been converted into actual ones. In other words, it was a network riddled with structural holes that were not spanned.

The Enterprise 2.0 Bull's-Eye

The concepts of interpersonal ties and structural holes provide a way to frame the benefits of Enterprise 2.0 and to show how popular ESSPs differ from one another. Consider the prototypical knowledge worker inside a large, geographically scattered organization (all of what follows also applies to smaller and more centralized organizations, but probably to a lesser extent). She has a relatively small group of close collaborators; these are people with whom she has strong professional ties. Beyond this group is another set of people—those she has worked with on a past project, coworkers with whom she interacts with periodically, colleagues she knows via an introduction, and the many other varieties of "professional acquaintance." In Granovetter's language, she has weak ties to these people.

Beyond *this* group is a still larger set of fellow employees who could be valuable to our prototypical knowledge worker *if only she knew about them.* These are people who could keep her from reinventing the wheel, answer her pressing questions, point her to exactly the right resource, tell her about a really good vendor or consultant, let her know that they were working on a similar problem and had made some encouraging progress, or perform any of the other scores of helpful activities that flow from a well-functioning tie. By the same token, if our focal worker is a person of goodwill, she could help many other people in the company if her existence, work experiences, and abilities were more widely known.

But because the structural holes between the focal worker and the members of this large group have not been spanned by a person, the interpersonal ties are only *potential*, not actual. The people remain unaware of each other and so can't put their nonredundant networks in contact with one another. While this may represent a hole-spanning opportunity for an individual within the organization, from the leader's perspective it's just a shame and a loss. The leader would prefer all networks to be interconnected, as long as it doesn't cost too much.

The bull's-eye diagram in figure 4-1 is an extremely simple representation, not to scale, of the relative size of these three groups—strongly tied colleagues, weakly tied colleagues, and potential ties—from the perspective of our focal knowledge worker. The small core of people with whom she has strong ties lies at the center, surrounded by her larger group of weak ties. Potential ties are in the third ring. My intuition says that for most knowledge workers the three circles in the figure are nested accurately—that the number of potential ties, say, is

FIGURE 4-1

Relative volume of different types of ties for a prototypical knowledge worker

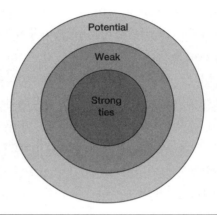

greater than the number of weak ties—even if their relative sizes are not accurate.

Poor Tools for Important Jobs

Research on weak ties, structural holes, and many related concepts within social network analysis has revealed the importance of the outer two rings of the bull's-eye. The ability to form, maintain, and exploit weak ties and the ability to convert potential ties into actual ones (either strong or weak) are both hugely valuable assets, both to individuals and to the enterprises in which they work. Our tendency to focus only on strongly tied colleagues within enterprises has given way to a broader and more useful perspective that encompasses weak and potential ties as well.

Until recently, however, few technologies were available to help people and organizations that wanted to adopt this perspective. Maintaining and exploiting weak ties and converting potential ones were human activities, conducted face to face or, more rarely, over the phone.

Earlier generations of IT helped with these activities, but not much (groupware and knowledge management were primarily intended for strongly tied colleagues). I often ask my students and audiences what pre-Web 2.0 technologies, if any, were available to help individuals keep their network of weak ties up to date on their activities. The annual family update letter that some people send out around the holidays is the best response I've heard. I also ask about the reverse challenge: keeping up to date on the news from one's entire network of weak ties. I have yet to hear of a good pre-Web 2.0 technology that addressed this need.

Finally, I ask about older technologies for *exploiting* a network of weak ties by, for example, asking all of its members a question and hoping for a quick and helpful answer. Many of my MBA students previously worked as analysts at large consultancies and banks. They have used blast e-mails, listservs, and group instant messaging to ping their networks of weak ties with questions like, "Has anyone sized the Eastern European 3G telephony market?" or, "How many public medical device manufacturers are there, and which of them are outperforming the market?" They reported varying levels of success and satisfaction with this method and also pointed out a few of its shortcomings. E-mails are often perceived as intrusions and ignored, while instant messages can easily be missed.

At the level of potential ties, the main drawback to human-based methods for converting them into actual ties is, essentially, that these methods don't go far enough, fast enough. Some of the people who span structural holes do so selfishly, with the explicit intent of getting paid or increasing their social capital, whereas others do so selflessly, aiming simply to connect people who otherwise wouldn't have met. But within any sizable enterprise many, if not most, holes remain unspanned. In order to span two nonredundant networks, a person must either already be a member of both of them or make the effort to become a member. Human network spanners, in other words, need to be both well positioned and motivated—typically a rare combination.

Enterprises have long realized both the value of converting potential ties into actual ones and the deficiencies of relying on human-based methods alone to accomplish this task. Consequently, they've experimented with a number of technological tools aimed at the third ring of the bull's-eye. These tools can be divided into three categories: directories, document repositories, and automated tie suggesters. *Directories* are essentially digital organizational white pages; they provide a listing for each person giving his or her contact data and other hopefully relevant information such as education, experience, and areas of expertise. Some of this information is generated automatically from the enterprise's human resources systems, while some can be entered by the people themselves. Directories can be useful, but I have yet to find a large company whose employees thought that its directory captured and displayed the "right" information about people. Rather, they regarded the directory pages like most other intranet pages: static, sparse, and often out of date.

Document repositories are common at organizations like law firms and consultancies, where almost all capital is human capital and all work knowledge work. This work is typically captured in documents, including presentations and spreadsheets, which are stored in searchable repositories. Many people report that these documents are valuable not primarily for their content, but for their authors. In other words, documents point to potential ties. Many current repositories, however, do not highlight this aspect of their documents and instead focus primarily on their content.

Automated tie suggesters are information technologies that monitor knowledge workers' computer activities (e-mail, Web surfing, and so on) for a time, identify people with similar patterns of activity, and then suggest to these people that they should form a tie. While these technologies show promise, they have not yet been widely implemented. Where they have, privacy concerns have often appeared. Many people do not want their online activities monitored and analyzed, even if it's being done with the best of intentions.

New Tools for Strongly Tied Colleagues

In fact, there are problems with the technologies used to support unstructured collaboration even at the innermost ring of the bull's-eye, where ties are strong. When I speak to or teach groups, I often ask people to raise their hands if they generate most of the documents they're responsible for with a group of collaborators, rather than individually. Typically, most hands go up; evidently few reports, spreadsheets, and presentations in enterprises these days are authored by just one person. I then ask people to leave their hands up if, when generating and refining these documents, they work primarily by attaching them to e-mails addressed to all collaborators. Again, with most audiences, most hands remain in the air. Finally, I ask people to keep their hands in the air if they're largely happy with this style of collaboration. Most hands come down.

Everyone who has collaborated this way is familiar with the two major challenges of version control and simultaneous editing. Version control refers to the fact that it's difficult to keep track of which version of the document is the current or "correct" one. Simultaneous editing, that is, two or more people working separately on the document at the same time, inevitably leads to incompatible versions that must somehow be reconciled, usually by painstaking, side-by-side comparisons. It's virtually impossible to prevent simultaneous editing when collaborators are all working with their own copies of documents, copies that have been sent to them as e-mail attachments.

Wikis, which elegantly address the challenges of version control and simultaneous editing, are effective tools to support the work of strongly tied colleagues. (The first wikis were for text editing, but wiki-like tools have also been developed for spreadsheets and presentations.)

Wikis solve the version control problem by keeping all contributions from all collaborators in one central repository, making it impossible for different versions to exist on the hard drives of individuals' computers. Simultaneous editing becomes an issue with a wiki only if it's truly simultaneous—if two people are editing the document at exactly the same time. There are a few approaches for dealing with this situation. MediaWiki, the wiki software that underlies Wikipedia, alerts users when they attempt to save the page they're working on and shows them the edits made by others since the last save. Google Docs, a wiki-like word processor from Google, comes close to showing others' edits as they happen.

At VistaPrint, the direct marketing company whose case study opened chapter 2, senior software engineering manager Dan Barrett employed a wiki to capture and spread knowledge.[7] To begin, he set himself the task of documenting everything a new technical hire would need to know in order to be effective within the company. He asked himself and his colleagues questions like, "What would an engineer need to know on day 1 here? Within the first week? During the first month?" As he listened to and recorded answers, Barrett drew up lists of knowledge topics such as department names and attributes of software used within the company.

After about three months he had identified approximately one thousand topics. Most of these topics were interrelated, so Barrett also kept track of many types of relationships, including similarities ("Computer" and "PC"), hierarchies ("Operating systems" and "Windows"), and more general associations ("World Wide Web" and "Browser"). He did *not* attempt to become an expert on all of these topics, or to define the content that should go within them.

Barrett knew that VistaPrint would use IT to help capture knowledge on these topics, but as he asked questions and built topic lists, he was *not* trying to design or specify any particular system. He was simply working to understand the knowledge a new technical employee needed to have, and how the bits and pieces of this knowledge related to one another.

During this process he came to believe that wiki technology was well suited to capturing and organizing knowledge among VistaPrint's engineers, in part because the philosophy underlying wiki contribution was similar to the company's approach to modifying code. As Barrett explained:

Lots of companies "lock down" their code bases and give only a few people the ability to make changes. We take a very different approach. Any of our engineers can "check out" a piece of code, then "check in" an updated and hopefully improved version. All of these actions are logged, so that if something stops working we know exactly who worked on it, or who worked on code that interacts with it, and when they did so. If necessary, we can always revert back to the previous version of the code—the one that was in place prior to the appearance of the problem. We believe that you ensure high code quality NOT by locking it down in advance, but instead by giving lots of people the opportunity to improve things while maintaining a tight audit trail.

Wikis work exactly the same way. Anyone can add something or change something, and all edits are tracked and can be reverted. Quality comes from letting lots of people contribute with few up-front rules, but maintaining the ability to see who did what, and undo anything that turned out *not* to be a good contribution. So wikis are a natural fit for us; they correspond well to the way we're used to working.

Barrett also liked a few other aspects of wikis. First, he considered them to be almost "frictionless" to use; a participant could add, edit, or search for information almost immediately, with very few steps or mouse clicks. He found that many other group-level technologies, in contrast, required their users to "jump through a lot of hoops" before they could do anything valuable. Second, he liked how participants could add structure to wikis by linking and tagging. Barrett had worked with many classic KM systems and felt that the hierarchical structure they imposed on all content was not appropriate for an organization's knowledge. Linking and tagging were not imposed and were not hierarchical; instead, they reflected people's understanding of how topics related to one another. Finally, he liked how wiki software such as MediaWiki (the application that Wikipedia was built on top of) could be integrated with other programs such as VistaPrint's bug-tracking software.

Barrett installed MediaWiki software at VistaPrint with the goal of getting the company's engineers to enter their accumulated knowledge into it. He knew, however, that it would be difficult to persuade these knowledge workers to take time out of their busy days to do so. To make it as frictionless as possible for them, therefore, he preconfigured the wiki with articles devoted to the thousand knowledge topics he had recorded and with links between those articles that reflected the relationships among them. The existence of predefined articles meant that someone with knowledge about "bug tracking" or "e-commerce Web site" would immediately know where to record this information. Engineers were free to modify or extend this initial structure, but Barrett felt that it was important for the wiki to *have* an initial structure.

He added no content to these articles himself. Instead, he encouraged his colleagues to do so. When he received an e-mail whose content was relevant to the wiki, he replied to the sender with a request to add that content to the wiki, including a link to the appropriate page. He found that people were almost always willing to take the couple of minutes required to put the information on the wiki, and in many cases even added to it. This content might not be beautifully formatted, but Barrett was not concerned about this. As he put it "information is more important than layout."

As the company's engineers kept adding content, Barrett assumed the role of editor in chief of the wiki—formatting contributions, moving content around, adding links and tags, and generally making sure that it was easy to read, navigate, and search. He found the combination of constantly nudging his colleagues to add content, then editing their contributions to be a powerful one. As the wiki grew, it became useful to the company's engineers, who in turn became more likely to contribute to it. This virtuous cycle led to rapid growth, and by the summer of 2008 the wiki had grown to include populated articles (ones with at least some text) on approximately eleven thousand topics. Employees had used tags to place these articles into more than six hundred categories, and Barrett believed that all of the company's engineers both used the wiki and had contributed content to it. Of the eleven thousand topics, he estimated that all but five were directly relevant to VistaPrint's business; the rest were social.

In August 2008 VistaPrint was ready to roll out use of the wiki well beyond the engineering department and to make it the knowledge repository for the entire company. Barrett was optimistic that this effort would be successful, even though the MediaWiki software did not support WYSIWYG ("what you see is what you get") editing and was therefore a bit more difficult to use than word-processing programs such as Microsoft Word. Initial experiments showed him that most VistaPrint employees could learn to edit effectively in MediaWiki, with about forty-five minutes of training. However, because most of these employees still did much of their work using programs such as Word, Excel, and PowerPoint, the company was also planning to deploy Microsoft's collaboration suite, called SharePoint.

New Tools for Weakly Tied Colleagues

Wikis and similar group-based technologies for creating and modifying documents are excellent technologies at the center of the bull's-eye, where collaborators are strongly tied. At each of the outer two rings of the bull's-eye, a different ESSP also becomes valuable. As the example of Serena software shows, social networking software (SNS) like Facebook is a powerful tool for connecting weakly tied collaborators and facilitating their interactions.

Serena, the company that was the subject of the second case study in chapter 2, used Facebook to help build a stronger and more consistent corporate culture. In October 2007 Serena decided to largely walk away from its current intranet and replace it with Facebook. The company did not abandon its intranet because of expense—the intranet leveraged Serena's own content management system and so was very cheap to maintain—but because it was static, dull, and not heavily consulted.

CEO Jeremy Burton and chief marketing officer René Bonvanie, who were heavy users of SNS on the Web, realized that it had just the opposite properties: it was dynamic, interesting, and addictive for many people. Facebook gave its users tools to assemble a network of people, stay on top of what these people were doing, and provide their own updates to the network. Serena's executives realized that these were just the activities needed to create a stronger sense of community within the company.

Serena held the first of its "Facebook Fridays" in November 2007. These voluntary sessions were intended to make employees comfortable with the software and its uses. Initial investigations had shown that people were particularly interested in pictures of their colleagues, since in many cases they had no idea what a coworker looked like. On the first Facebook Friday people were encouraged to bring their digital cameras and come to work dressed in a way that showed something about themselves. Burton, an automobile racer, dressed in his racing suit, while

CFO Robert Pender arrived in golf clothes. People in the offices took pictures of one another and uploaded them, while those who worked from home dressed up and took pictures of themselves; within twenty-four hours, more than half the company's employees had pictures as part of their Facebook profile.

Serena did not build or buy a private version of Facebook; instead, it used the standard public application available on the Web. However, many employees wanted to keep at least some of the information in their profiles private and unavailable to everyone on the Internet. To educate the workforce about Facebook's privacy tools and options, the company brought in to its larger offices teenagers (usually the children of employees) who were expert Facebook users to conduct training and answer questions.

After the pictures were up, the most commonly used Facebook feature at Serena was the status update, which allowed users to post a short message about what they were doing. This update was then made visible to all members of the user's network. As vice president Kyle Arteaga explained:

> At any given time I know as much about my colleagues as they want to share via Facebook, for example John B. from IT "is sucking on a starbucks, yummy," and Peter S. from Support "is gesturing evily at the rain clouds."
>
> So I now have context when I next speak to each of them. I actually need to call John about a project we are working on later today and I will bring up his Starbucks comment. Peter and I work together quite a bit and he is based in London, so having lived there recently I can commiserate with him about the weather.[8]

Facebook use contributed to the broader goal of introducing Serena's workforce to Web 2.0 and its culture of openness and information sharing. Unless employees used the site's privacy tools to keep information hidden, all that they posted for their colleagues was also visible to all Facebook members throughout the Internet. Arteaga explained the rationale for this:

> We want customers, vendors, partners, prospective em-
> ployees, and anyone else who is interested to be able to
> easily find out more about our company. We want to be
> approachable and find that the best way to do this in
> today's world is through viral means . . .
>
> We share the belief that work and home lives are
> starting to become very intertwined. The separation
> that used to be prevalent is becoming less and less so
> with the ubiquity of BlackBerrys, mobile phones in
> general, and social networking sites. This is why we en-
> courage employees to determine for themselves what
> their level of comfort is with this increasing trans-
> parency (e.g., learn how to create slices of your profile
> so that you share the right information with the right
> people). We also realize that many (particularly millen-
> nials) only know complete transparency, and that with
> complete transparency the traditional buttoned-down
> corporate culture that has thrived for so long may well
> be dismantled . . .
>
> Concern[s have come up] about questionable post-
> ings on people's profile and/or related Facebook blogs.
> While we can certainly see why people might take of-
> fense at certain topics and/or opinions, we have not
> changed our communications policy despite our social

networking initiatives. At the end of the day, we trust our employees to use common sense. We consistently tell them "be smart, do what you think is right." Of course, everyone's parameters are different. But we see no reason why we should put out specific Facebook guidelines on what you can and can't post, it's not as if we put out guidelines on what people say on the weekend at their neighbor's barbecue or at their child's piano recital.

Facebook participation was voluntary, but became quite widespread at Serena. By the end of 2007 the company estimated that 90 percent of its employees had created a profile. Approximately 25 percent of Serena's Facebook users were active, meaning that they visited the site multiple times a day, while another 50 percent accessed Facebook at least three times a week.

In 2008 the company began using Facebook to host videos and other materials related to its marketing campaigns and to announce, popularize, and recruit for its corporate social responsibility efforts such as Green Day and Children in Need.

In September 2008 Arteaga reported on some of the concrete benefits arising from Serena's heavy use of Facebook:

We are holding our annual user event next week . . . Normally we have five hundred people in attendance. This year attendance is double.

The main reason for this is Facebook. While our traditional customer base is still coming, we were able to extend to a much wider set of interested parties by exclusively using social networking. We asked employees to put links to the event in their status updates for the past month, we asked them to post the conference site in their profile and to join the conference group.

As a result we have five hundred new attendees, all friends of friends of friends. Not a single traditional email or outbound call went out to solicit this new group . . .

On top of this, we have also received many resumes of interested job seekers. In fact, I received my job via Facebook over a year ago. Our former head of sales recruited me when he found out [via Facebook] that I was leaving [my previous job]. Several of my colleagues were hired in similar fashion. And of course, quite a bit of networking has taken place via Facebook at all levels. Our head of support regularly converses with his support peers in other companies through a Facebook group he started.

Facebook was not the first SNS on the Web, and several other social networking tools are currently available. Some of them, such as LinkedIn, are specifically intended for business purposes. So why did Serena choose Facebook? Facebook has a few attributes that combine to make it particularly appropriate for the second ring of the bull's-eye, which contains large numbers of weakly tied collaborators.

First, it can "hold" large numbers of weak ties for each user. Facebook calls each contact a friend, and members can easily accumulate hundreds or even thousands of friends. Members can search their list of friends to find a specific person and then go to that person's profile page for contact data and any other information they've decided to post. In short, Facebook serves as a large and rich address book for weak ties.

Second, it lets members post many kinds of update, which it then communicates to friends. All Facebook members have a status field, which is simply a short text box. Members can type whatever they want in this box and change it as often as they like. The snippets of information from coworkers that Kyle Arteaga cited in the Serena case study—including "is sucking on a starbucks, yummy" and "is gesturing evily at the rain clouds"— are examples of status updates. Facebook members can also post photos, videos, links to Web pages, longer notes, and other types of content and pointers to online content.

These same features mean that Facebook is a tool members can use not only to update their friends but also to stay in touch with what all of these friends are doing. In other words, the site is not just for broadcasting, but also for receiving many individuals' broadcasts. All members' home pages center on a chronological list of all their friends' updates, with the most recent at the top. A quick perusal of this list lets users know what their friends are doing.

The activities of both broadcasting and receiving on Facebook are technically trivial for users, and quickly accomplished. It takes no skill and very little time to update and share information with friends, and to find and consume this information. As a result, an SNS like Facebook holds out an intriguing promise: the ability to let people build larger social networks than would otherwise be possible.

In a series of articles in the early 1990s, the anthropologist Robin Dunbar compared data about the neocortex (a region of the brain) volumes of various primates with the maximum sizes of their social groups. The two were tightly related, causing Dunbar to hypothesize that "animals cannot maintain the cohesion and integrity of groups larger than a size set by the information-processing capacity of their neocortex." He used the primate data to estimate the theoretical maximum social group size for humans, calculating that it was somewhere between 100 and 230, with a most likely value of 150. "Dunbar's number," as this has come to be known, represents a ceiling on the number of people with whom an individual can maintain stable social relationships. As Dunbar put it, "The figure of 150 seems to represent the maximum number of individuals with whom we can have a genuinely social relationship, the kind of relationship that goes with knowing who they are and how they relate to us. Putting it another way, it's the number of people you would not feel embarrassed about joining uninvited for a drink if you happened to bump into them in a bar."[9]

By reducing the amount of time and effort required to track other people's social activities, an SNS can potentially increase the number of people with whom one can have a true social relationship. As Carl Bialik reported in a November 2007 post to his *Wall Street Journal* blog, "Dunbar . . . says that [social-networking sites] could 'in principle' allow users to push past the limit. It's perfectly possible that the technology will increase your memory capacity," he says.[10]

Some people, of course, are not comfortable sharing all of their SNS information and updates with their entire network, and Facebook's core concept of friends is in some ways incompatible with hierarchical relationships within an enterprise; a boss, after all, is not the same thing as a friend. Facebook, however, has many different privacy settings, which allow users to control the information that they share and receive. Teenagers, with their active and fluid social lives, are often quick to master these settings, which explains why Serena asked the children of some of its employees to lead training within the company on privacy and SNS.

Facebook currently lets members ask their network a question and collects the answers on one globally visible page. I imagine that successful enterprise Facebook equivalents will have more advanced tools to allow members to exploit their networks actively by asking them for assistance in many different ways. I also imagine that they'll let users post answers to their most frequently asked questions and then simply point seekers to this resource.

It seems clear that Facebook and similar technologies, when deployed within an organization, blur the border between an individual's personal and professional lives. This border will have to be negotiated and monitored as enterprise SNS becomes more popular. Serena's approach was to encourage employee participation, to set few hard-and-fast rules, and to leave most decisions in the hands of the individual. To date, the company has been pleased with the results of this approach. Because Serena grew by acquisition and is geographically highly dispersed, most of its employees are only weakly tied. The company has found the Internet's freely available SNS extremely well suited to maintaining and often strengthening these ties. Facebook, in essence, did what the company's own intranet couldn't do; it helped knit the enterprise together more tightly.

New Tools for Converting Potential Ties

ESSPs have also knit the U.S. intelligence community more tightly together by converting some potential ties into actual ones. In chapter 2 the case study of the IC's failure to connect the dots prior to 9/11 closed with the announcement of the Galileo Awards, an initiative to surface new and innovative ideas. The winner of the first Galileo Award was "The Wiki and the Blog: Toward a Complex Adaptive Intelligence Community," by Calvin Andrus, the chief technology officer of the Center for Mission Innovation at the CIA. As Andrus's paper pointed out:

> The value of a knowledge-sharing Web space (wiki and blog) grows as the square of the number of links created in the Web space. There is knowledge not just in content items (an intelligence cable, for example), but also in the *link between* one content item and another—a link, for example, from a comment in a blog to an intelligence cable. Think of the value of a blog that links a human source cable to an intercept cable to an image cable to an open source document to an analytic comment within the context of a national security issue. When such links are preserved for subsequent officers to consider, the value of the knowledge-sharing Web space increases dramatically. When 10,000 intelligence and national security officers are preserving such links on a daily basis, a wiki and blog system has incredible intelligence value . . .
>
> Once the Intelligence Community has a robust and mature wiki and blog knowledge-sharing Web space, *the nature of intelligence will change forever* . . . The Community will be able to adapt rapidly to the dynamic national security environment by creating and sharing Web links and insights through wikis and blogs (emphasis in original).[11]

In another paper that won an honorable mention in the Galileo contest, Defense Intelligence Agency (DIA) analyst

Michael Burton stressed the value of free and easy platforms for contribution, and mechanisms such as linking to let structure emerge and improve navigability.[12]

In an article in the *New York Times Magazine*, writer Clive Thompson presented a scenario for how ESSPs could have helped prevent the 9/11 attacks:

> With Andrus and Burton's vision in mind, you can almost imagine how 9/11 might have played out differently. In Phoenix, the F.B.I. agent Kenneth Williams might have blogged his memo noting that Al Qaeda members were engaging in flight-training activity. The agents observing a Qaeda planning conference in Malaysia could have mentioned the attendance of a Saudi named Khalid al-Midhar; another agent might have added that he held a multi-entry American visa. The F.B.I. agents who snared Zacarias Moussaoui in Minnesota might have written about their arrest of a flight student with violent tendencies. Other agents and analysts who were regular readers of these blogs would have found the material interesting, linked to it, pointed out connections or perhaps entered snippets of it into a wiki page discussing this new trend of young men from the Middle East enrolling in pilot training.
>
> As those four original clues collected more links pointing toward them, they would have amassed more and more authority in the Intelink search engine. Any analysts doing searches for "Moussaoui" or "Al Qaeda" or even "flight training" would have found them. Indeed, the original agents would have been considerably

more likely to learn of one another's existence and perhaps to piece together the topography of the 9/11 plot. No one was able to prevent 9/11 because nobody connected the dots. But in a system like this, as Andrus's theory goes, the dots are inexorably drawn together.[13]

The IC already had an intranet environment well suited to deploying ESSPs like wikis and blogs. This environment was actually a group of networks, each open to people with the appropriate security clearances. Construction on these networks was begun in 1994, and by early 2005 separate top secret, secret, and unclassified networks spanned all the agencies of the IC (these networks were separate from each other for security purposes). Google's search technology had been deployed across all of these networks by that time.

In early 2005 Andrus spoke about his ideas to a group of analysts who advised the CIA on technology issues. Sean Dennehy, a member of that group, was skeptical about the value of ESSPs for intelligence analysis but decided to investigate them. After spending time on Wikipedia, he was impressed by that community's ability to generate accurate and valuable information, to discuss the process of generating that information (these discussions were captured in the "talk" page that was part of each article), and to keep a record over time of all of its work (Wikipedia's underlying MediaWiki software, like most wiki applications, archives a copy of every version of every page). Dennehy felt that good intelligence analysis required exactly these capabilities, as well as greater collaboration than had historically been the case within the IC.

Dennehy and Andrus approached the director of national intelligence (DNI)'s Intelligence Community Enterprise Services

(ICES) group, which was already seeking approval to have MediaWiki software deployed at each of the three levels of security throughout the IC. Dennehy worked on Iraq issues, but he saw that it would be counterproductive for the IC to have separate wikis for each topic, or indeed for each agency. He and Andrus instead advocated for something very much like Wikipedia: a single wiki with pages devoted to any and all topics of interest. DNI/ICES, essentially an IT support organization, needed champions within the mission areas of the IC to test out and advance the new capability. Dennehy and Andrus willingly agreed to play this role. The ESSP resulting from these interactions, called Intellipedia, was prototyped in November 2005 and officially announced to the IC in April 2006.

Communitywide blogs had been launched in March 2005. One of Don Burke's colleagues read a blog entry about the nascent Intellipedia in early 2006 and mentioned it to him. Burke, who worked in the CIA's Directorate of Science and Technology, had independently reached many of the same conclusions as Andrus and Dennehy about the shortcomings of current approaches to analysis and how to address them. The 130th person to edit Intellipedia, he quickly came to see the technology's potential. He and Dennehy interacted and collaborated using the wiki for several months. Even though both were longtime CIA employees and worked in the same building, they had never met and did not know each other before using Intellipedia.

By April 2006, Burke and Dennehy had been freed of their other duties to concentrate on popularizing and curating Intellipedia. They began to travel frequently, speaking to interested decision makers and groups about Intellipedia and the IC's other ESSPs. They also established a five-day sabbatical program for analysts interested in learning how to use the new technologies. In their sabbatical curriculum and presentations the two Intelli-pedians stressed three core principles:

- *Work at the Broadest Possible Audience.* To respond to the DNI's "Responsibility to Provide" guidance, it is imperative that we challenge ourselves to work in the collaborative space with the broadest possible audience. We define "broadest possible audience" by the broadest network to which an individual has single-click access. Where sensitivity issues start presenting themselves, we encourage building "basecamps" of information in the broader audience and then only moving in to more restrictive space for the sensitive information. This is feasible with these tools because of the ease with which users can create links between the environments . . . a process we call creating "breadcrumbs." The network can then control access. If an interested party has access, they will be able to follow the link. If they don't, they at least know more information exists and they can begin following the breadcrumb if it is important enough for them to do so.

- *Work Topically, Not Organizationally.* This principle should be applied when the article is first given a title and every time a contributor edits the page content. When working topically, each organization can add what they know to a common page. So instead of having a CIA page on Fidel Castro and an NGA page on Fidel Castro, we simply have an organizationally neutral page called Fidel Castro onto which everyone contributes their information.

- *Replace Existing Processes*. We are all very busy and we
  don't have time to take on new duties. We advocate that
  individuals and organizations look for processes that
  they can replace with these new tools. For instance,
  users must compile and synthesize a lot of information.
  Instead of the traditional process of working individually to gather their data in personal shared drives, folders, and work documents, they can replace that process
  by working in the wiki. Instead of using email to debate
  an idea, they can use blogs. Instead of using their
  browser's "favorites" list, they can use social tagging.
  Instead of storing files in a shared folder behind a firewall that is not indexed by search engines, they can use
  Inteldocs. This is called moving from "channels" to
  "platforms." A platform is a shared space where information can be easily linked, searched, tagged, etc. So,
  when a new analyst comes onboard and are asked to
  write about insurgency, they can find previous discussions and debates on the topic.[14]

Over time other ESSPs, in addition to blogs and Intellipedia, were deployed across the IC. These included applications for sharing and commenting on photos and videos, and
for adding tags to online content. Because of the IC's unique re-
quirements for functionality and security, these pieces of software were developed internally.

In February 2008 the Knowledge Laboratory of the DIA
published observations and conclusions resulting from a set of
fifteen interviews conducted with agency analysts about their
use of Intellipedia and the IC's other ESSPs. It concluded,
"The results suggest that Intellipedia is already impacting the

work practices of analysts. In addition, it is challenging deeply held norms about controlling the flow of information between individuals and across organizational boundaries." One interviewee said that "[We] are seasoned enough to know this isn't just a piece of software—this could change the way we're doing business, and to me this is the antithesis of the way we used to do things."[15]

Although the Intellipedia wiki is probably the IC's best-known social software, blogs have also been important, particularly at the third ring of the bull's-eye. Just as SNS strengthens weak ties, blogs have several properties that make them well suited for converting potential ties into actual ones. First, they are easy to update; it takes little time and virtually no technical expertise to create a new post. This allows people to, in the words of blog pioneer Dave Winer, "narrate their work"—to describe what they're doing in a way that's not burdensome, yet is instantly and universally visible.

Second, most modern blogs are configured so that each update, also called a *post*, can be viewed or referenced as a separate Web page (an attribute called *permalinking*). So while a blog usually appears as a long page of short posts, it's also a collection of many short pages, each one constituting a post. This means that if I want to refer to another blogger's work when I'm writing my own blog, I can be quite precise. I don't have to link to the blog as a whole; I can instead link to exactly the post of interest, even if it's only a sentence or two in length.

Finally, blogs are permanent collections of posts. Even though all posts aren't always visible on the main page, they do not vanish or expire, but persist over time. They can be located by people and search engines, and links to them continue to work.

Because of these properties, a blog is well suited to capturing whatever a worker wants to record and broadcast over time. This can include both the process and the output of knowledge work—finished products (reports, analyses, conclusions, and so on) as well as the efforts that went into generating them. It can also include commentary, opinions, questions, stray thoughts, and the like. The blog itself is indifferent across these different types of post. Chapter 6 takes up the question of whether the enterprise as a whole should also be indifferent, or whether giving workers freeform platforms for self-expression involves substantial risks. For now, let's assume away any such risks.

These properties make it easy for a group of bloggers to refer and point to one another's work via links, since these will be both precise and permanent. A set of tightly interlinked blogs has two desirable properties. First, it's easy for a person to navigate—to follow a theme, debate, or train of thought across many blogs by clinking on their links. Second, and perhaps even more important, modern search engines such as Google's rely heavily on links. As discussed in chapter 3, links on the Web provide strong indicators of quality and relevance, and Internet searching improved dramatically with Google's PageRank algorithm. Intranet searching can see parallel improvements if intranet content becomes heavily interlinked and if search engine technology similar to Google's is deployed. Enterprise blogs can help fulfill the first of these two conditions.

And what's the benefit to an enterprise of having a densely interlinked Intranet? Well, one clear advantage is that any particular piece of online content becomes easier to find via search. But Euan Semple, the manager responsible for the BBC's early and successful adoption of ESSPs, stressed that too strong a focus on making content such as corporate documents easier to find can obscure deeper benefits. As he wrote in a blog post,

> With a few rare exceptions, once you found the document it was likely to be badly written, barely relevant and out of date . . .
>
> I came to believe that what people really wanted was to find someone who knew what they were talking about. Even if that "knew what they were talking about" meant knowing which document to read, why and where it was to be found. So what we did was start building online social spaces like forums, blogs and wikis in which highly contextual, subjective, complex patterns and information could start to surface about anything and everything in the business that was interesting and worth writing about.
>
> The result was that when someone said on our forums "I need to find the official documentation on x because I am about to do y" they were usually rewarded, and very quickly, with multiple answers along the lines of "Well I found this document answered my questions because . . . " pointing them at the documentation. Indeed increasingly the source they were directed to was a blog or a wiki containing up to date, contextualized information.
>
> Having context in the question, context in the answer and the collective memory of your corporate meatspace, empowered by the mighty hyper-link, in between is hard to beat.[16]

The Urban Dictionary defines *meatspace* as "referring to the real (that is, not virtual) world, the world of flesh and blood. Somewhat tongue-in-cheek. The opposite of cyberspace."[17] Semple used this word to stress that answers in the BBC's online forums came from other employees, not from effective searches of digital documents. This ESSP, in other words, was valuable not because it connected people with information, but because it connected people with other people who possessed information.

The experience of the IC and Enterprise 2.0 is similar in many ways to that of Semple and the BBC.

Many intelligence analysts have found that the greatest value of the IC's ESSPs, including blogs, is their ability to connect people who would otherwise have remained isolated from one another. I saw this phenomenon at work during my own research on Enterprise 2.0 within the IC. Don Burke asked me to send him questions for analysts, which he then posted on his internal blog. The first of these was, "What, if anything, [do the] Enterprise 2.0 tools let you do that you simply couldn't do before? In other words, have these tools just incrementally changed your ability to do your job, or have they more fundamentally changed what your job is and how you do it?"

Most of the responses to this question stressed the ability of ESSPs to convert potential ties into actual ones, as well as the novelty and value of this ability:

> *From a DIA analyst:* "These tools have immensely improved my ability to interact with people that I would never have met otherwise. I have been working with the IC advanced R&D offices . . . since 1999, so my job was always about networking and exchanging information since DIA does

not do its own internal R&D. I learned to value networking and worked extensively with representatives from industry, academia, think tanks, and IC R&D members. But it was still hit or miss as to who I would meet and how far I would get into their knowledge base (especially if tacit). In many cases, I couldn't access anything digitally but was dependent on finding an e-mail or a phone number from someone in the IC in order to make contact . . . Enterprise 2.0 tools have helped considerably in exposing new information, new projects, and bringing new thought leaders . . . to the forefront. People that would never have been visible before now have a voice . . ."

From an NSA analyst: "Before Intellipedia, contacting other agencies was done cautiously, and only through official channels. There was no casual contact, and little opportunity to develop professional acquaintances—outside of rare [temporary duty] opportunities, or large conferences on broad topics. Tracking down a colleague with similar mission interests involved finding reports on Intelink or in our databases, and trying to find whoever wrote them. But establishing a rapport or cultivating exchanges of useful information this way was unlikely at best.

After nearly two years of involvement with Intellipedia, however, this has changed. Using Intellipedia has become part of my work process, and I have made connections with a variety of analysts outside the IC. None of the changes in my practices would have been possible without the software tools . . . I don't know everything. But I do know who I can go to when I need to find something out. Broadening my associations outside my office, and outside my agency, means that when someone needs help, I am in a better position to help them get it."

From an NSA engineer: " . . . there's now a place I can go for answers as opposed to data. In addition, using that data and all the links to people associated with that data, I can find people who are interested in helping me understand the subject matter. Since I've been involved in Web 2.0 activities, I have met many new people throughout the IC. They are a great resource for me as I continue my career. Their helpful attitude makes me want to help them (and others) in return."

From a DIA scientist: "IC blogs allow me to connect to people that I would not otherwise know about. I can see what they are working on, and use it to make a real introduction."

From an NSA analyst: "More importantly, I am no longer writing to satisfy my immediate supervisor, or even a single 'customer.' Nor I am relying on one person's view of what is 'needed' by the customer. By interacting with the whole community—even those outside my target set—I am learning where my products fit in the greater scheme of the IC, and can tailor my activities to produce intelligence of the greatest value to the broadest possible audience."

From a CIA analyst: "The first aspect that comes to mind when I contemplate how these tools have improved my ability to do my job is the ease of shar[ing] ideas and working collaboratively with intelligence professionals around the world . . . without leaving my desk. This is probably an incremental change—although a huge increment—because I could always do these things to a certain extent using traditional techniques (e.g. the telephone).

On the other hand, I am actively involved in an early stage project that would be impossible without these tools. The ability to link information and people together, as wikis and blogs do, makes possible an activity that I truly believe will transform our Community. The tools fundamentally altered the course of this project. I know that my example is only one of many similarly transformational activities that are germinating or will germinate when these tools reach a greater level of penetration of the IC workforce."

From an NSA analyst: "Wikis and blogs have changed my work life significantly. It's extremely useful to be able to post a question on my blog if I get stumped, go and work on something else, and then come back to the problem and read my peers' responses. Usually I can pull a solution from them, which saves me time and general aggravation/hassle."

These responses are obviously a biased sample and can't be assumed to represent the views of the IC as a whole, but they do illustrate the ability of ESSPs to convert potential ties into actual ones.

New Tools for Interactions Between Strangers

In the Google case study in chapter 2, Bo Cowgill was interested in building a prediction market within the company but unsure how to proceed and who to work with on the project. So he used a simple social software platform that worked at the third ring of the bull's-eye. When he returned from vacation after reading *The Wisdom of Crowds*, he wrote the following note on an internal online message board where employees could post their new ideas:

> By aggregating the number and nature of incoming links to a webpage, Google already uses the collective genius of crowds to rank search results. "Democracy on the web works," is part of our corporate culture. But PageRank isn't the only way to harness the collective intelligence of large groups.
>
> The Iowa Electronic Markets, the Policy Analysis Market, the Hollywood Stock Exchange as well as numerous academic studies have shown that large, diverse crowds of independent thinking people are better at predicting the future or solving a problem than the brightest experts among them. This is especially true when the individuals in the crowd have a personal financial stake in getting it right.
>
> Google has exactly what such a market needs to perform well: A large, diverse user base and the ability to give financial incentives and lower barriers to entry. To some extent, Google can even ensure that our crowd thinks independently.
>
> So, I propose creating Google Decision Markets . . . who wants to work on it with me?[18]

All Google engineers had "20 percent time," the equivalent of one day a week during which they were free to pursue projects of interest within the company that were not directly related to their jobs. Cowgill was hoping to convince some Googlers to devote their 20 percent time to building a prediction market. He was also looking for quick feedback about the idea, and the message board let people rate posted ideas. As figure 4-2 shows, most respondents thought Cowgill's idea was a good one.

Ilya Kirnos posted a reply less than ten hours after Cowgill submitted his idea: "Hey Bo, I had a similar idea and have written some code in that direction. I agree that markets have a lot of predictive power, much more so than surveys or polls for most things . . ."[19]

Kirnos saw that Cowgill's proposed prediction market could be used to accomplish many of the same objectives as his betting system and volunteered to help with the project, thereby converting a potential tie into an actual one. Two other Googlers

FIGURE 4-2

Responses to proposal for a Google prediction market

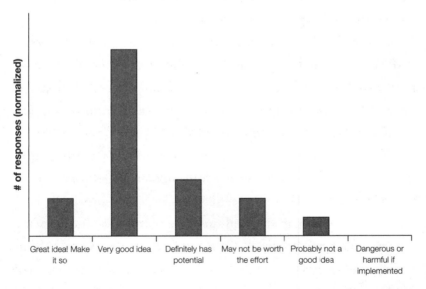

Source: Peter Coles, Karim Lakhani, and Andrew McAfee, *Prediction Markets at Google*, Case no. 607-088 (Boston: Harvard Business School Publishing, 2007).

also replied to Cowgill's post and became part of the prediction market's team.

Another respondent to Cowgill's post was an associate of Hal Varian, a well-known Berkeley economist who consulted at Google. The respondent told Cowgill that Varian had an interest in prediction markets and had written about them in his *New York Times* economics column. Cowgill contacted Varian to solicit his help, and Varian began attending the group's regular meetings. He later offered crucial advice about how to design the markets, how to implement them, and how to popularize them within the company.

After finalizing the market design, the newly formed team started programming, and completed a working version of a prediction market in less than a month. The team then decided to seek more formal support and recognition from Google, as well as funding for rewards. Some successful initiatives, including Google News and the AdSense advertising sales program, had started as employee proposals.

Cowgill's proposal for "Google Prediction Markets" (GPM), which he submitted in December 2004, received favorable reviews and sparked interest among several executives. One of them committed to providing $10,000 from his department's budget each quarter to fund GPM prizes.

During its first quarter of operation, which ran from April through June, there were twenty-four markets (questions) within GPM and ninety-five total different securities (answers) being traded. The team had decided on these markets by interviewing Google managers to find events of interest that would occur during the quarter. These included when a specific international Google office would open and how much demand there would be for a particular product. The team also created markets based on the company's list of important corporate objectives, updated each quarter. In addition, the team included markets for events that would occur outside the company, such as product launches by a competitor. Finally, GPM also contained "fun" markets related to events such as the opening of the movie *Star Wars: Episode III*, the television reality show *The Apprentice*, and the NBA finals. Fun markets were intended to draw in participants and show them how easy and enjoyable it was to trade. All markets were open to all employees once they opened an account, and all Googlers could browse the markets and see their current prices and price histories, even if they didn't have a GPM account. A randomly selected market appeared prominently on Google's intranet. GPM documentation included an overview and list of frequently asked questions.

During the first quarter, 1,085 Googlers signed up for a trading account within GPM. A total of 7,685 trades were made, and 436,843 shares changed hands. Most of the traders came from the engineering, sales, operations, or product management functions within the company.

As data accumulated, the prediction markets team started to analyze it to learn how the markets were working, and how well. One of the main areas of interest to them, of course, was the accuracy of the markets—how well they forecast what would actually happen.

To assess accuracy, Cowgill took the final prices for a large sample of outcomes in GPM and divided them into ten ranges: 0.0–0.1, 0.1–0.2, and so on up to 0.9–1.0. If these prices really were equivalent to probabilities that the events would occur, he reasoned, outcomes priced between 0.0 and 0.1 should occur somewhere between 0 and 10 percent of the time in the real world. In a large enough sample, they should occur on average 5 percent of the time.

FIGURE 4-3

Price versus percentage winners

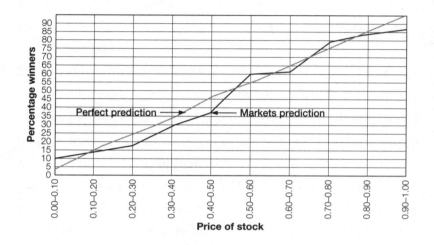

Source: Peter Coles, Karim Lakhani, and Andrew McAfee, *Prediction Markets at Google*, Case no. 607-088 (Boston: Harvard Business School Publishing, 2007).

Cowgill compared real-world outcomes to GPM prices for each of the ten price ranges. As figure 4-3 shows, final market prices were, in general, good probability estimates.

Analyses also revealed that at every point in time, even as much as ten weeks away from the closing date of the market, the most expensive outcome was the one most likely to actually occur (see figure 4-4). It seemed that GPM's markets, in other words, could quickly and accurately distinguish among possible outcomes, identify the one most likely to occur, and attach a high price to that outcome.

Google's prediction markets shared with all markets a fundamental property: the ability to generate highly valuable information by bringing together people who have little or nothing in common. This property of markets was highlighted by the

FIGURE 4-4

Average price of winning and losing stock

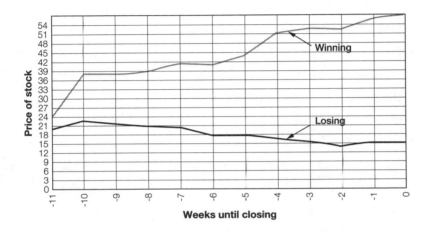

Source: Peter Coles, Karim Lakhani, and Andrew McAfee, *Prediction Markets at Google*, Case no. 607-088 (Boston: Harvard Business School Publishing, 2007).

Austrian economist Friedrich Hayek in his seminal 1945 article "The Use of Knowledge in Society." Hayek focused attention away from markets' wealth-generating properties and concentrated instead on their ability to aggregate and transmit useful information in the form of prices:

> The . . . problem of a rational economic order is . . . that the knowledge . . . of which we must make use never exists in concentrated or integrated form but solely as the dispersed bits of incomplete and frequently contradictory knowledge which all the separate individuals possess. The economic problem of society is . . . a problem of the utilization of knowledge which is not given to anyone in its totality.

We must look at the price system as such a mechanism for communicating information if we want to
understand its real function . . . The most significant
fact about this system is . . . how little the individual
participants need to know in order to be able to take the
right action . . . It is more than a metaphor to describe
the price system as a kind of machinery for registering
change, or a system of telecommunications which enables individual producers to watch merely the movement of a few pointers, as an engineer might watch the
hands of a few dials, in order to adjust their activities to
changes of which they may never know more than is
reflected in the price movement . . .

The marvel is that in a case like that of a scarcity
of one raw material, without an order being issued,
without more than perhaps a handful of people
knowing the cause, tens of thousands of people
whose identity could not be ascertained by months
of investigation, are made to use the material or its
products more sparingly; i.e., they move in the right
direction . . .

I have deliberately used the word "marvel" to shock
the reader out of the complacency with which we often
take the working of this mechanism for granted. I am
convinced that if it were the result of deliberate human
design, and if the people guided by the price changes
understood that their decisions have significance far beyond their immediate aim, this mechanism would have
been acclaimed as one of the greatest triumphs of the
human mind.[20]

In his 2006 book *The Undercover Economist*, journalist Tim Harford provided a concrete example of the marvel Hayek described:

> [In a perfectly competitive market] every product would be linked to every other product through an ultracomplex network of prices, so that when something changes somewhere in the economy (there's a frost in Brazil, or a craze for iPods in the US) everything else would change—maybe imperceptibly, maybe a lot—to adjust. A frost in Brazil, for example, would damage the coffee crop and reduce the worldwide supply of coffee . . . In Kenya, coffee farmers would enjoy bumper profits and would invest their money in improvements like aluminum roofing for their houses; the price of aluminum would rise and so some farmers would wait before buying. . . .
>
> That may seem like a ridiculous hypothetical scenario. But economists can measure and have measured some of these effects: when frosts hit Brazil, world coffee prices do indeed rise, Kenyan farmers do buy aluminum roofing, the price of roofing does rise, and the farmers do, in fact, time their investment so that they don't pay too much. Even if markets are not perfect, they can convey tremendously complex information.[21]

The examples of markets in general and prediction markets in particular indicate that the Enterprise 2.0 bull's-eye should have a fourth ring—one that encompasses people who are neither current nor potential ties. In figure 4-5 this new outermost

FIGURE 4-5

Relative volume of different types of ties for a prototypical knowledge worker, updated

Updated to include people with whom the prototypical worker will not ever form a tie; these people are within the ring labeled "None." Prediction markets are an ESSP that allows untied people to interact.

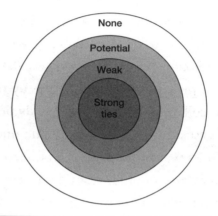

ring is labeled "none," and the people in it are not necessarily ever going to form valuable ties, either strong or weak, with our focal knowledge worker; they are professional strangers. All the people in this ring, however, can productively interact with one another in markets, and in doing so they can generate valuable information in the form of prices.

The traders in Google's market and in Internet prediction markets such as the Iowa Electronic Market and the Hollywood Stock Exchange have demonstrated an ability to collectively generate accurate predictions about a wide range of events. The technologies they use to do this have all of the attributes of an ESSP. Trading in a market is very similar to the activities of linking and tagging described in chapter 3; they are all self-interested individual actions that yield substantial group-level benefits. Corporate prediction markets like the one at Google are ESSPs that can be productively used by people who are strangers—and will remain so.

The complete four-ring bull's-eye picture shows that Enterprise 2.0 is valuable at any level of tie strength, from strong to nonexistent. The four case studies presented at the outset of this book were arranged by ring, starting at the innermost with VistaPrint's close colleagues and moving out to untied traders in Google's prediction market. I arranged them this way to illustrate that the prototypical ESSP differs by ring, with wikis for strongly tied collaborators, SNS for weakly tied ones, a blogosphere to convert potential ties into actual ones, and prediction markets for untied people. These tools can, of course, be valuable at other rings as well; strongly tied colleagues, for example, can all trade in a prediction market, and the Intellipedia wiki has helped intelligence analysts convert potential ties into actual ones. I place them at different rings of the bull's-eye in order to stress that the various ESSPs are *not* all essentially the same, and that they don't all do the same things or have the same effects when deployed within an organization. Instead, they are useful in quite different ways at each successive ring of the Enterprise 2.0 bull's-eye.

5

Uniquely Valuable

The Benefits of Enterprise 2.0

I n addition to being useful at different levels of tie strength, emergent social software platforms (ESSPs) are also used by organizations for different purposes. A wiki, for example, is different from a prediction market. What's more, the same tool can be used in multiple ways; blogs can be used to broadcast answers *or* questions. So in addition to understanding the bull's-eye model of tie strength, it's also important for business decision makers to understand the range of benefits that the new social software platforms can provide.

This chapter describes the advantages of Enterprise 2.0. It concentrates on the valuable capabilities that can be acquired with ESSPs, and that are impossible, or at least very difficult, to acquire without them.

The Enterprise 2.0 bull's-eye shows that ESSPs can be useful at levels of tie strength ranging from high to nonexistent. As the discussion in the previous chapter also revealed, the new social software platforms can be used for a variety of purposes. A wiki, for example, is used by small or large groups of people, who may be strongly or weakly tied, to create a document or Web site collaboratively. A tagging tool like Delicious, meanwhile, is also used productively by people at many tie strengths, but for a purpose other than document creation. So in addition to emphasizing the usefulness of Enterprise 2.0 at different levels of tie strength, it's also important to emphasize the breadth of benefits that ESSPs offer to organizations that adopt them successfully. Once decision makers understand what these benefits are, they will be well positioned to decide whether to pursue Enterprise 2.0, and if so which tool(s) to deploy.

I define Enterprise 2.0 benefits as those that arise from the deployment and use of ESSPs and that are difficult to achieve otherwise. These benefits, in other words, don't arise readily from using previous generations of collaboration technology, or no technology at all. I've observed six such benefits: group editing, authoring, broadcast search, network formation and maintenance, collective intelligence, and self-organization. These benefits are described in more detail below, along with the ESSPs most closely associated with each one.

Group Editing

Group editing simply means the ability of a diverse set of people to collaborate on a single, centrally stored work product: a document, spreadsheet, presentation, or Web site. As discussed above, modern ESSPs such as wikis and Google Docs and Spreadsheets address the problems of version control and simultaneous editing that hamper many efforts to generate a work product as a group.

These ESSPs are also inexpensive (many of them, in fact, are currently free to use) and require users to have no specialized software beyond a Web browser. As browsers become more powerful, and as the developers of wikis and other group editing tools improve their offerings over time, we can expect that the differences between using these tools and using stand-alone software for word processing, spreadsheets, and the like will shrink. Group editing, in other words, will come to look and feel more and more like today's individual knowledge work.

Group editing is sometimes most valuable at the center of the bull's-eye, where collaborators are strongly tied colleagues. In many organizations I'm familiar with, this is the main thrust of Enterprise 2.0 efforts. These organizations establish group editing environments for all entities (labs, workgroups, business units, client teams, and so on) that want them, or let the entities set them up for themselves. In most cases these environments are closed, that is, nobody outside the predefined group can edit content, and the content is invisible outside the group.

There may be valid reasons, including security and confidentiality, to make group editing environments closed by default, but this approach has two disadvantages. First, inaccessible content can't be searched, linked to, or tagged, and so can't be useful to anyone outside the group. The second disadvantage is the inverse of the first one: not only is it impossible for inaccessible content to be useful to outsiders, it's equally impossible for outsiders to contribute any useful content. Closed group editing environments are often set up to mirror and support what the sociologist Etienne Wenger has termed "communities of practice," or organizational groups with a shared goal.[1] These communities, which are important for generating and sharing knowledge and educating new members, can be surprisingly powerful.

It would seem natural and smart to set up a group editing environment for each community of practice, and this is exactly what many organizations have done. One of the earliest and best-known examples was the Eureka system, established to support knowledge sharing among Xerox repair technicians.[2] It also seems natural, or at least not harmful, to close the ESSP so that only community members have access to it. As already noted, however, doing so prevents people *outside* the community from making contributions that might be valuable *within* the community; it removes, for example, the possibility that a Xerox salesperson, or supplier, or customer could use the Eureka system to help the copier technicians solve a problem or alert them to an important issue.

When it's at least somewhat difficult or expensive to establish a large-scale digital platform to support group work, it probably does make sense to keep platforms small and match them to communities of practice. But when it's trivially cheap and easy to set up unlimited digital platforms, it's often beneficial to do so, for the simple reason that helpful ideas and other innovations can come from anywhere. As MIT's Eric von Hippel writes in his book *Democratizing Innovation*:

> But if, as we have seen, the information needed to innovate in important ways is widely distributed, the traditional pattern of concentrating innovation-support resources on a few individuals is hugely inefficient. High-cost resources for innovation support cannot efficiently be allocated to "the right people with the right information": it is very difficult to know who these

people may be before they develop an innovation that turns out to have general value. When the cost of high-quality resources for design and prototyping becomes very low (the trend we have described), these resources can be diffused very widely, and the allocation problem diminishes in significance. The net result is and will be to democratize the opportunity to create.[3]

In short, it may seem logical to make group editing ESSPs closed environments, but decision makers should keep in mind that doing so removes the chance of valuable contributions from outer rings of the bull's-eye.

Authoring

Authoring, in this context, means generating content and putting it online for a broad audience. Unlike sending an e-mail or using any other channel technology, authoring is a public act. Authoring can take many forms, from sharing status updates using social networking software (SNS) to posting photos, videos, and podcasts to writing a blog.

For enterprise purposes, the clearest value of blogging and other forms of authoring is sharing knowledge, expertise, experience, and insight in a way that's both persistent and easily consultable. When enterprise authors link to one another's content, when users tag this content, and when 2.0-era search technology is deployed that surfaces the most relevant content in response to a query, the primary goal of the knowledge management movement can be realized: the organization generates a dynamic repository that contains much of what it "knows," and members can both produce and consume the contents of this repository over time.

An example from the Canadian real estate development company Intrawest Placemaking shows how valuable authoring can be. In April 2006 the company added authoring software called ThoughtFarmer (developed by OpenRoad Communications) to its intranet, giving all employees the ability to create blogs and other content.

At the online repository of Enterprise 2.0 case studies, cases2.com, ThoughtFarmer co-creator Chris McGrath wrote:

> By turning every user into a contributor, OpenRoad envisioned several benefits for Intrawest Placemaking:
>
> *Fewer barriers to knowledge sharing.* By letting users publish their own content with only a few clicks, they would be less likely to hoard knowledge and more likely to share it.
>
> *No distortion in knowledge transfer.* Ideas would be exchanged person-to-person, in one step, eliminating distortion and filtering.
>
> *An increase in employee engagement.* Users that could add and edit content would feel a sense of ownership over their intranet. Because the leadership of Placemaking would be putting considerable trust in employees, employees would, in turn, be more likely to trust the company and its leaders.
>
> *Self-healing content.* If a user saw an error, he or she would be able to fix it immediately, reducing inaccuracies.

No excessive burden on a couple of administrators. The users would be the editors. Content maintenance would no longer require a dedicated team.

The principal community-building feature of ThoughtFarmer is "Place" pages: a personal area where each employee can add a profile, upload photos and documents, create pages, and share favourite links. Every change an employee makes to the intranet—every comment posted, every file uploaded, every page added—has the employee's name by it, linked back to his or her "Place." Other employees can follow the links, learn about each other, explore each other's content, and develop relationships . . .

Mike Hartigan, a Placemaking project manager in Vancouver, was overseeing the construction of a 66,000 square foot, heated tile entranceway for a new condo-hotel. The project would traditionally have required the radiant subcontractor to return for each of the 33 concrete pours to lay piping amongst rebar. Then Hartigan had an idea: instead of laying tile, just complete the slab, lay all the radiant piping on top, apply a two-inch layer of coloured concrete with an aggregate, and then polish it.

Hartigan's innovative method saved $500,000 on a $2 million job, improved coordination among the trades, reduced the project timeline, and gave a stunning, better-than-tile appearance. Hartigan then created a page about his experience on the Thought Farmer–powered intranet. Other project managers in Florida and Nevada posted comments to the page, asking further questions. In response, Hartigan posted photos of the finished job and addressed their comments. Other construction managers planned to use the technique on future projects.

Placemaking manages dozens of multi-million dollar developments a year. As Hartigan's technique is implemented, Placemaking will save millions of dollars. Without Placemaking's everyone-as-editor collaboration system, ideas such as Mike's could never have been shared in such a discoverable, accessible, permanent format.[4]

Broadcast Search

The inverse of authoring is *broadcast search*, where people publicize not what they know, but instead what they don't know. Broadcast search is the posting of queries in a public forum in hopes of receiving an answer. It is not a recent phenomenon. In 1714, for example, the British government publicly announced a large cash prize to anyone who could find a way to accurately determine the longitude of a ship at sea (a challenge eventually met by the Yorkshire clockmaker John Harrison).[5]

Computer networks and ESSPs, however, have greatly expanded the frontiers of broadcast search. On the Internet popular volunteer forums like Yahoo! Answers exist, as do for-profit ventures such as Innocentive, a clearinghouse for scientific problems and problem solvers. Research groups within large organizations use Innocentive to post descriptions of scientific problems that have them stumped. These problems are "anonymized," assigned a solution value of between $2,000 and $105,000, and then made available over the Web to the more than 80,000 independent scientists from over 150 countries who have an account with Innocentive. A 2007 study by Karim Lakhani, Lars Po Jeppesen, Peter Lohse, and Jill Panetta, found that 29.5 percent of 166 problems posted to Innocentive had been solved.[6]

As with group editing, the chances of serendipity with broadcast search increase as more and more people are brought into the community and invited to examine the problem and contribute solutions. Lakhani and his colleagues found, for example, that the most important factor in determining whether a problem posted on Innocentive was solved was the diversity of scientific interests among people around the world who examined it.

At Google, Bo Cowgill broadcast his search for collaborators on a prediction market throughout the company; he did not limit his queries to his strongly tied coworkers. The team that eventually formed to develop and oversee the market was composed of people from several different functions, few of whom knew one another before responding to Cowgill's broadcast search. As discussed earlier, Euan Semple began Enterprise 2.0 at the BBC with online question-and-answer forums open to the entire organization. He realized the power and attractiveness of broadcast search.

Network Formation and Maintenance

The examples of Serena software and the popularity of Facebook, LinkedIn, and their peers show that ESSPs can also provide the benefit of *network formation and maintenance*. Social software platforms are clearly collections of information, and as a result many people commonly think of them primarily as reference works like encyclopedias. The example of Wikipedia reinforces this perception. As discussed in chapter 4, however, insights from the U.S. intelligence community and Euan Semple's experiences at the BBC show that ESSPs do not just capture what people know—they also point to people themselves.

Within enterprises, most contributions to ESSPs can be traced back to their author (in contrast to the Internet, where contributions are often anonymous). This feature allows a searcher or browser to quickly identify people who could be valuable or helpful colleagues, based on their online track record. The searcher can then initiate contact with this person, and so convert a potential tie into an actual one. Whether or not these newly tied colleagues use an ESSP like a wiki or SNS software for their subsequent interactions, ESSPs deliver value in this example simply by bringing people into contact with one another. The new software platforms, in other words, span structural holes and help people build up valuable social networks over time.

Some of these platforms are dedicated to helping people maintain and exploit these networks. Facebook and other SNS applications keep people up to date on what both their strongly and weakly tied colleagues are doing. This capability is particularly valuable for weak ties, which can fade over time if they're not maintained. SNS makes this maintenance task almost effortless; users simply provide updates about themselves that are then automatically and immediately broadcast throughout the network to strong and weak ties alike. I imagine that future versions of enterprise SNS will incorporate deeper capabilities for authoring and broadcast search, making it trivially easy, for example, for a knowledge worker to ask her network a question and collect answers.

One of the deep insights underlying the shift from Web 1.0 to Web 2.0 was the realization that software should be social— that in addition to making individuals more productive and automating away their roles in a process, software could and should also be used to let people find one another and form communities. At present social networking software is the purest expression of this insight. It seems very likely that social software will continue to evolve, both on the Internet and within and between enterprises, providing even more ways for people to find and interact with one another.

Collective Intelligence

Collective intelligence, or the wisdom of crowds, refers to the use of technologies like prediction markets to generate answers from a dispersed group. Very often these answers are better—more accurate and more decisive—than answers obtained through traditional individual or small-group methods. There is ample evidence that tools like prediction markets work well, and I expect that they will become more popular over time within enterprises, just as SNS software will.

Collective intelligence is also used by many Web sites to identify "good" content. Some of these sites, such as the news aggregator Digg, do this by explicitly asking users to vote. Others, such as Amazon, observe how shoppers navigate and behave. These shoppers aren't making any explicit recommendations, but as a group they do make implicit ones. When I'm shopping for electronics, for example, Amazon often tells me what other people ultimately buy after viewing the same item I'm looking at. If 35 percent of them buy a USB drive other than the one I'm looking at, I'm likely to click on that other drive to see why it's so popular. In this case, a form of collective intelligence has helped me make my purchasing decision.

Self-Organization

Perhaps the broadest benefit from social networking software and other ESSPs is *self-organization,* or the ability of users to build valuable communities and resources and shape them over time, without having to rely on guidance from any center or headquarters. I find this the most remarkable property of Enterprise 2.0, and also the easiest to overlook. We learn to take the phenomenon of online emergence for granted so quickly that we fail to stop and reflect on how remarkable it is that many uncoordinated low-level interactions can result in the appearance of high-level patterns and structure.

Google search results, Delicious tag clouds, networks of strong and weak ties captured within SNS, and many other aspects of Web 2.0 and Enterprise 2.0 are at once commonplace and extraordinary. They all spring from the work of individuals, and although this work is often spontaneous, uncoordinated, and self-interested, it nevertheless yields resources and environments that appear highly planned, predefined, and coordinated by some authority.

It's probably safe to say that self-organization is not a concept that comes naturally to most enterprises. After all, one of the key features of every enterprise is hierarchy, or a predefined and largely stable structure. Within a classic hierarchy, attributes like authority, expertise, and role are assigned or conferred. Responsibility for innovation lies within the R&D department, for example. Everyone within the hierarchy can point to the R&D department as the place where innovation happens, and it happens there because that's where the people who know the most about innovation work. These people are assumed to know the most about innovation because of their education, prior experience, and other credentials that could be assessed at the time they were hired.

Organizations that pursue Enterprise 2.0 do not have to disband their R&D departments or any other element of their existing hierarchy. But they do to some extent have to let go of the notion that attributes like authority, expertise, and appropriate roles should be specified up front and never again questioned. They need to replace this notion with the idea that expertise, authority, and role are (at least in part) emergent over time, rather than fully specified in advance. They can then deploy ESSPs and let their people interact with one another to determine who knows what and who should work together, rather than having these decisions always defined or made by managers up front. Fundamentally, I believe that the enterprises deploying ESSPs to best advantage will be those that see self-organization as a deep benefit, rather than a risk.

Just as organizations don't have to operate within only one ring of the bull's-eye when pursuing Enterprise 2.0, they also don't have to pick just one of the benefits described here. Although these benefits are categorically different, they are not either-or propositions. It's perfectly possible, for example, to simultaneously establish ESSPs to support authoring *and* network formation and maintenance. I have described the benefits individually here for the same reason that I divided the bull's-eye into separate rings: to help decision makers think through what Enterprise 2.0 should mean for their organization and how it can be most valuable. Should Enterprise 2.0 mean giving strongly tied colleagues better tools for group editing? Should it mean giving authoring tools to all employees, or setting up a broadcast search capability? Is collective intelligence the main goal?

Clarity about goals brings clarity about means—the tools that an organization will acquire and deploy, and the steps it will take to ensure broad and deep adoption. One of the questions I hear most often from managers in organizations both large and small, public and private, is, "We want to pursue Enterprise 2.0—how should we start?" I respond by asking them to talk a bit more about what they mean by Enterprise 2.0 and by introducing the concepts of the tie strength bull's-eye and the set of possible benefits. I have found that these frameworks help focus the discussion about ESSPs for the enterprise in productive ways. This discussion of goals soon leads to a conversation about adoption—how to make sure that the new technologies are accepted and used productively. The rest of this book considers the issues surrounding ESSP adoption.

Part II

SUCCEEDING WITH ENTERPRISE 2.0

6

Red Herrings
and Long Hauls

*What Is, and Isn't, Difficult About Adopting
the New Tools and Approaches*

T his chapter looks at the principal challenges of Enterprise 2.0, the main obstacles to an organization's successful deployment of emergent social software platforms (ESSPs).
I have noticed an interesting pattern: before an organization begins an Enterprise 2.0 effort, its leaders typically have a consistent set of concerns about the negative things that could
happen. But most of these are not real or serious risks—I call
these *red herrings*.

After an organization begins to deploy ESSPs, its leaders'
concerns often shift to one simple issue: *How can we go faster?* They

are often surprised by the fact that Enterprise 2.0 is a long haul and puzzled that the effort is not progressing more quickly.

   This chapter first examines why so many initial concerns are actually red herrings and then explains why deployment of ESSPs is a long haul.

Red Herrings

I've noticed that concerns around Enterprise 2.0 fall into two broad categories: fears that people won't use the newly available ESSPs, and fears that they will. The latter, which stem from the lack of upfront control common to ESSPs, tend to crop up first. When first exposed to these technologies, business decision makers voice concerns about what happens when direct control is surrendered and many people can freely contribute to information platforms. The scenario of broad participation in these platforms behind the firewall gives rise to a consistent set of worrying questions:

   What if employees use their internal blogs to post hate speech or pornography, or to harass a coworker?

   What if blogs are used to denigrate the company itself, air dirty laundry, or talk about how misguided its leadership and strategy are?

   What if nasty arguments break out in a discussion forum and the whole thing descends into name calling and "flame wars"?

   Won't people be tempted to use forums to talk about current events, review movies, ask for advice about camcorder purchases, and have other non-work-related conversations?

What if people waste time filling up their employee profile pages with pictures of their kittens and vacations?

Will people just use social networking software to plan happy hour, rather than to get work done?

Don't Enterprise 2.0 platforms yield just another source of discoverable content—material that must be turned over as part of a lawsuit or other legal action?

If the information on these platforms really is valuable, won't it be harvested by spies and sold to the highest bidder?

Won't hackers break into our Enterprise 2.0 platforms and steal their content?

Don't these technologies make it easier to leak secrets, deliberately or inadvertently, to the outside world?

Don't they make it too easy for confidential information to leap over our internal Chinese walls?

If we give up tight control over our intranet's content, how can we possibly avoid running afoul of all potentially relevant regulations and laws on information sharing in all the places we do business?

The list of concerns grows when an organization also considers extending Enterprise 2.0 tools and approaches to external groups such as prospective customers, actual customers, suppliers, and other community members:

What if unhappy customers use our community site to air their grievances, and to talk loudly and often about our lousy products or Kafkaesque customer service?

What if a supplier uses our site to complain about how we never pay on time?

Are we responsible and liable if people give incorrect information or bad advice on question-and-answer forums we host on our Web site?

This is a daunting list, and many companies conclude that whatever the benefits of Enterprise 2.0, it's not worth running the array of risks indicated by these questions. I've heard from many executives that their legal and human resources departments have advised against pursuing Enterprise 2.0. (To be fair, I've also heard that some companies' human resources departments are big supporters of the new tools and approaches.) And for many decision makers, risks and nightmare scenarios seem concrete and immediate, whereas benefits appear more nebulous and distant. In such cases Enterprise 2.0 never gets off the ground; company policies become hostile to freeform information sharing and the technologies that support it, and incipient efforts are shut down.

Whenever I'm doing research or consulting at a company that's been pursuing Enterprise 2.0 for a while, I ask about horror stories—the worst things that have happened related to use of the new technologies. I also often solicit such stories when I speak at conferences. And I keep my eyes open for catastrophes in the blogs, sites, magazines, and journals that I read. In short, I have made a serious effort to collect examples of counterproductive, dysfunctional, or risky consequences of Enterprise 2.0. Yet my collection is almost empty. I have yet to come across *any* true horror stories—scenarios that make me question whether the risks associated with deploying ESSPs actually do outweigh the benefits.

To understand why this is, let's first place the concerns listed above into a few categories and then examine how the technologies, communities, and leaders of Enterprise 2.0 have been able to address them effectively. There are a few legitimate risks associated with deploying ESSPs, but far fewer than most people expect.

The first and largest category of risk is *inappropriate behavior and content*, either deliberate or inadvertent. As the list of questions above indicates, widespread concern exists that people will use ESSPs to post content that is offensive, alienating, needlessly provocative, irrelevant, or otherwise out of line with the goals of the organization.

All Internet surfers have at some point come across Web content that they found offensive or disturbing, and many online communities and discussions seem to be dominated by trolls, which Wikipedia defines as people who post "controversial and usually irrelevant or off-topic messages in an online community, such as an online discussion forum or chat room, with the intention of baiting other users into an emotional response or to generally disrupt normal on-topic discussion."[1] It seems quite possible that trolls and offensive content would also eventually appear on an organization's internal ESSP. In other words, if a company tried to make its intranet multivoiced and egalitarian (as the Internet is), some of these voices would be unpleasant enough to drive others away, and perhaps even to land the company in trouble for offenses like creating an environment of harassment in the workplace. Four factors, however, combine to make this scenario unlikely.

First is the fact that while anonymity is the default on the Internet, on the intranet attribution is the norm. People can launch blogs, post comments, and edit wikis on the Internet without revealing their identities, but in most internal corporate ESSPs it's possible to tell who made each contribution. Some companies have allowed unattributed employee comments on certain blogs, but this is as much anonymity as commonly exists on intranets. When attribution is the norm, people are much more likely to be cautious and circumspect, and much less likely to "flame" their colleagues. And if workers do misbehave on an ESSP, they can be easily identified, counseled, educated, and disciplined if necessary.

The second factor limiting inappropriate behavior is self-policing. Participants in an ESSP usually come to feel a sense of community and are therefore quick to react when they feel that a member is violating community norms. Counterproductive contributions are often met with a flurry of messages and posts that highlight why the content was out of bounds, reiterate norms, and offer corrections. The communities formed on top of ESSPs often have informal leaders who exert a great deal of influence and can shape the behavior of other members.

In addition to informal leaders, the formal leaders of an organization are a third counterbalance to inappropriate behavior and content. Managers can intervene when one of their direct reports is being counterproductive in an ESSP, and often the simple awareness that "the boss" is observing behavior and watching contributions leads to changed behavior.

I saw this firsthand recently on the wiki I set up for my MBA students. Contributions to this wiki were responsible for one-half of their grades, but I gave them very little upfront direction except to say that they should look at the wiki as an online textbook for the course that they would write collaboratively during the semester. My goal with this assignment was, of course, to have students experience emergence for themselves. This semester, as is often the case, students set up discussion boards within the wiki in order to set norms and policies and talk about what the textbook should look like.

My policy was to contribute to this ESSP as little and as rarely as possible; I told students that it was their resource, not mine. As I watched during the early part of the semester, though, I saw that some of the discussions were in danger of descending into a *flame war*, which the online dictionary webopedia.com defines as a series of "posts or messages in a thread that are considered derogatory in nature or are completely off-topic. Often these flames are posted for the sole purpose of offending or upsetting other users. The flame becomes a flame war when other users respond to the thread with their own flame message."[2] A few of my students were acting inappropriately and threatening to weaken the ESSP and its community.

I posted the following to the discussion:

> We need to constantly watch to make sure that our
> online discussions with each other don't ever become
> too hostile, dismissive, provocative, argumentative-for-
> argumentativeness's-sake, etc. By this point in your
> MBA careers, you have an excellent template for inter-
> acting with each other—the in-class discussion. A good
> ground rule is that if you read aloud a comment you're
> about to post, and find that it would sound "off" if said
> within an HBS classroom during a case discussion,
> don't send it. Please keep in mind that any wiki contri-
> butions that would have the effect of *discouraging* others
> from reading or participating in an online discussion
> are contributions that work *against* the goal of the tech-
> nology itself, and will be evaluated accordingly. Also

keep in mind that it's often hard online for others to tell
if you're kidding or joking or giving a real-world friend
a hard time; because text-only comments have little
context, they're easy to misinterpret. This is *not* to say
that online debate is bad; it's actually necessary and
healthy. It's just to say that we all need to pay particular
attention to the tone of our online discussions, and
strive here at least as much as in the classroom to be
courteous and respectful.

This comment showed that I was paying attention, and my
students certainly understood that the word *evaluated* is, in this
context, very close to *graded*. The flame wars stopped quickly.
I've had to intervene like this only once in the three years I've included a wiki in my course.

The fourth, and most fundamental, factor limiting inappropriate behavior and content is simply that most people know
how to behave appropriately in ESSPs and are inclined to do so.
They have well-formed notions of how to interact productively
with other community members, and they know what kinds of
content and contribution are out of bounds. There are exceptions, of course, and in a few instances people have been fired
because of ill-advised posts to their external blogs; but my experience indicates that most people know how to act professionally
in job-related environments, including digital ones.

I discovered evidence to this effect in late 2007 when I was
teaching a group of senior human resources executives from
very large organizations about Enterprise 2.0. One of the participants told a revealing story. Her company, which employed a
lot of young people, had become concerned about how the firm
was being discussed and represented in these employees' blogs,

MySpace pages, Facebook profiles, and so on. So she and some colleagues decided to have a look at all these environments.

She soon learned that many of the young employees mentioned their company as part of their digital identity, but virtually always in appropriate ways. The worst offense she found, after a *lot* of looking around, was a photo of a training session in which account numbers were visible on a blackboard. It turned out that they were dummy account numbers and that the person who posted the photo, when made aware of the concern, immediately apologized and took it down.

If a company believes that these four factors do not provide enough protection against inappropriate content, it can set up a review or moderation process in which contributions must be vetted before they appear on a content platform. This precaution is more common on externally facing sites, where vandals and spammers can wreak havoc. Finally, inappropriate content on company-owned ESSPs, either internal-only or externally visible, can always be removed if necessary.

Another common concern is that people will contribute *inaccurate information* to ESSPs. In this scenario contributors are not deliberately doing anything inappropriate; they're just misinformed. This concern is particularly acute for companies that host communities on their public Web sites in which participants can ask and answer questions. Wrong answers in such forums could at a minimum hurt the company's reputation, and could also lead to further problems.

As with inappropriate behavior, self-policing is often an effective antidote to inaccurate information. Community members, it seems, take it upon themselves to highlight and correct inaccuracies. There are few topics about which correct information is more important than in tax law, so this might seem to be an area where individuals would be better served by hired experts rather than a broad and unscreened community. Yet the financial software company Intuit has added a community to its Web site for TurboTax, its popular tax preparation application.[3] The experiences of many other companies that run community sites—including Dell, Cisco, Amazon, and many others—are similar: community members themselves do a thorough job of policing inaccurate content, which can be easily corrected or removed.

A closely related concern is the appearance of *embarrassing information* on an ESSP. This problem often takes the form of negative reviews of a company's products or services by a customer, or a more general expression of displeasure or distrust. Negative reviews on a community site sound like unambiguously bad news, but they can actually be beneficial in two ways. First, they help assure readers that the site has not been whitewashed of all negative content—that instead of containing only advertisements and cheerleading, it actually includes a more representative range of viewpoints. Negative reviews, in other words, increase confidence that positive ones can be trusted.[4] Second, negative reviews and comments call attention to problems, giving the company the opportunity both to become aware of them and to address them. In class discussions on this topic someone always makes a comment like, "Doesn't a smart company *want to know* about negative customer experiences as soon as possible? Community sites sound like great early warning systems." In addition, these sites allow companies to respond directly, quickly, and publicly to the person posting the embarrassing information. If the "service recovery" is an effective one, the community will see this. The cable television company Comcast has begun using Twitter both to scan for customer complaints about its service and to respond to them.[5]

Embarrassing information is not limited to external community sites; platforms behind the firewall can also contain information that some would prefer to keep hidden. I once visited one of the world's largest technology companies to talk with the people who were responsible for deploying ESSPs, including internal employee blogs. On the intranet page that listed the most recent blog posts I saw a title along the lines of, "Why Our Recently Announced Strategy Is Misguided." A little surprised, I asked the team if this level of dissent was rare, and if the people who wrote such posts found themselves in hot water.

They assured me that the answer to both questions was no. For this company, visible employee disagreement with official strategy was *not* embarrassing; it was welcome. It helped surface potentially important issues and made sure they were discussed.

One of my MBA students saw something similar at his summer employer, disguised here as "Chemco." In response to a class assignment question about the benefits of Enterprise 2.0, he wrote:

> I have been an eyewitness of the power of enterprise 2.0 (although I didn't know that is what it was called at the time) technology in promoting collaboration and connectedness across disparate individuals and groups within organizations. While interning at Chemco this summer, we were briefed on the Company's brand-new intranet, which included blogging capabilities. The site was relatively new, and only a few people (mostly more senior leaders) had created blogs at that point. About a month into the internship, my supervisor (the head of corporate development and strategy) forwarded us a link to one of the comments to the CEO's blog.

The comment had come from a low-level marketing manager located in a satellite office. In his remarks submitted to the CEO's blog, the marketing manager openly questioned Chemco's sacred cow—its ability to wring costs out of a process and to successfully operate an ultra-lean efficient organization. Specifically, he questioned the importance of one of the company's favorite metrics (something they are extremely proud of); I'll call it Metric A.

In his post (which was several pages, probably 800-plus words), he broke down basic financial information for Chemco and its 3 or 4 main competitors. Chemco was the clear leader in Metric A. He then overlaid this analysis with metrics such as market cap per employee and other metrics of value (I have forgotten what else he used), where Chemco was a distant laggard.

He went on to say that Chemco needed to essentially reverse its strategy and begin adding significant additional costs in the form of additional sales reps and R&D professionals, which are the key drivers of value in large chemical firms. His analysis was insightful, extremely thorough, and bold.

I was amazed at how much buzz it created in the organization—my project team decided to use much of his material as a source reference for one of our deliverables. The office of the chief executive formed a small (informal) task group to investigate some of the marketing manager's claims and test their potential benefit.

In short, without this new E2.0 vehicle, this manager's voice would likely never be heard. From the look of his robust analysis, this was something he wanted to (and perhaps had tried to) share for a long time, and he now had the means of doing so. As the above example illustrates, I think that the potential benefits of E2.0 to an organization can be revolutionary—a step-function improvement in collaboration and efficient dissemination of information and resources.

Many decision makers are concerned that ESSPs raise the risk of *noncompliance* with laws, regulations, or policies. These platforms have many contributors, wide borders, and little, if any, up-front verification of content. Furthermore, all contributions are instantly and widely visible, which seemingly increases potential harm, exposure, and liability. If employees deliberately or inadvertently post information that violates the laws or regulations in *any* environment where the company does business, there could be serious consequences.

I first thought of these risks as I was conducting interviews for the first Harvard Business School teaching cases I wrote on Enterprise 2.0. These cases were set at the European investment bank Dresdner Kleinwort Wasserstein (DrKW), and focused on the use of blogs and wikis. DrKW CIO JP Rangaswami had led the effort to deploy these technologies throughout the bank at a single point in time, to make them available to most employees, and to refrain from issuing detailed guidelines or policy statements about their appropriate uses.[6]

New York Attorney General Eliot Spitzer had recently made headlines for his successful prosecution of multiple U.S. investment banks, showing that some of their analysts had expressed pessimism about certain stocks in private to their colleagues while remaining optimistic about the same companies in comments to the public. There had also been high-profile cases about bank employees sending sensitive information over the Chinese walls set up to ensure that traders cannot gain access to nonpublic data about deals in progress.[7]

As I was interviewing Rangaswami, it occurred to me that ESSPs were hugely risky and inappropriate technologies for investment banks, especially as they were being implemented at DrKW. These tools spanned the firm's Chinese walls and provided forums for employees to voice their opinions behind the firewall; if these opinions were at odds with public statements, the bank could face serious penalties. And because DrKW did business in many countries, it was subject to a large and constantly shifting set of laws and regulations that could be difficult to monitor. I asked Rangaswami how he could possibly justify deploying ESSPs in such an environment, especially without issuing clear and detailed policies or conducting extensive training.

I found his response illuminating:

> These technologies are our best defense against financial industry regulators and prosecutors around the world. These parties don't typically come after you for isolated incidents or honest mistakes—they come after you for long-term patterns of misbehavior or illegal activity. And because our blogs and wikis are open to almost everyone, that means that everyone in the bank can be on the lookout for these patterns. As soon as anyone sees anything troubling on one of these platforms they can alert our compliance department, which can then take action. If there is a problem, we can show any regulator exactly what happened and when, when we became aware of it, the corrective actions we took, and whether or not the inappropriate activity stopped.

Now, contrast that with e-mail and instant messaging, our two most popular collaboration technologies at
present. We keep a record of all of this traffic over time
and we have the right to read it, but we can't possibly
monitor it comprehensively. And because e-mails and
IMs are invisible to everyone except the senders and
receivers, the bank's workforce can't look at them and
help us spot inappropriate activity. Keep in mind that
Spitzer used e-mail records to show that the analysts he
prosecuted were saying one thing in public and something very different in private. When I think about
compliance issues email makes me very nervous, and
blogs and wikis calm me down.[8]

I found Rangaswami's answer very insightful, and his argument very compelling. He helped me understand that ESSPs
actually reduce noncompliance risks, because their content is so
widely visible. Channel technologies like e-mail, on the other
hand, are risky because they are so private.

Rangaswami made another interesting point during the interview. He stressed that DrKW's workforce had been amply
educated about inappropriate behaviors and communications
in the workplace prior to the deployment of ESSPs, and so
could be trusted to use them properly. Employees who engaged
in harassment or violated Chinese walls, he said, would already
have been counseled or released, and it made no sense to him to
think that people were just waiting for Enterprise 2.0 technologies to appear so that they could start misbehaving.

Some of the questions listed earlier in this chapter reflect
concerns about *theft*, either by insiders who could copy content
from ESSPs or outsiders who might hack into the platforms to

steal content. Theft is always a possibility with digital informa-tion (indeed, with *any* information an organization possesses), but the platforms of Enterprise 2.0 seem to provide particularly rich targets because they aggregate many types of content. In other words, if it's true that ESSPs centralize and distill previ-ously disparate information and let the cream rise to the top, it should also be true that they contain content that would be highly valued outside the organization.

When assessing the magnitude of risks like theft and compar-ing them with the benefits offered by Enterprise 2.0, I find it particularly valuable to look at organizations where the risk is greatest. These organizations provide critical cases, and if they've decided that the benefits outweigh the risks, I conclude that the same is probably true for most other organizations as well.

I have trouble imagining that information theft can be more harmful anywhere than in a national intelligence agency. Yet the U.S. Directorate of National Intelligence (DNI) has supported Intellipedia and the other Enterprise 2.0 technologies that have been deployed across the sixteen federal agencies making up the nation's intelligence community (IC). Despite the relatively recent counterintelligence examples of Aldrich Ames at the CIA and Robert Hanssen at the FBI, both of whom were convicted of selling highly sensitive secrets to other countries, the DNI has concluded that the benefits of better and wider sharing of intelligence information outweigh the risks.

It's particularly interesting to note that the IC has not devel-oped all of its ESSPs internally in order to ensure that they are secure. Instead, it has deployed a number of publicly available applications, including a blogging engine from WordPress, the MediaWiki software that underlies Wikipedia, and a Google appliance for enterprise search. The first two of these are open source applications; the third is a commercial product. This evidence indicates that publicly available technologies can be secure enough even for highly sensitive environments. The critical case of the IC therefore indicates to me that the benefits of Enterprise 2.0 outweigh the theft risks for the great majority of organizations.

Whatever the advantages of Enterprise 2.0, though, it is true that ESSPs typically do increase the amount of discoverable information within an organization. In other words, they add to the inventory of material that can be requested and reviewed as part of a legal action, just as e-mails and memos can. Many organizations understandably want to limit the amount of discoverable information they produce, but they also want to gain access to the advantages and capabilities of Enterprise 2.0 as described in this book. Because I have yet to hear of a case in which ESSPs and their content gravely hurt a company during a legal proceeding, I continue to believe that the benefits of Enterprise 2.0 outweigh the potential disadvantages associated with generating more discoverable content. For most organizations, in fact, I believe that these benefits outweigh *all* the risks described above.

Long Hauls

The questions discussed earlier in the chapter came from managers in organizations that hadn't yet begun to deploy ESSPs. Once a company has made the decision to pursue Enterprise 2.0, the people in charge of the deployment usually ask a very different question: how can we persuade more of our people to use the new technologies? Many internal champions are frustrated by what they see as the slow pace of adoption within their organizations. In a common scenario a company, division, or work group installs one or more ESSPs, alerts its employees about them, conducts training, and then sits back to reap the benefits described in earlier chapters.

I thought I'd observe just this scenario unfolding at one of the first companies where I did research on Enterprise 2.0, a large financial services firm. One of the effort's champions was a line manager who wanted to take advantage of the benefits of group editing and self-organization. He became aware of the firm's wiki deployment and encouraged the people who worked for him to use it for their group-level work. However, it proved difficult to persuade his staff to use the new tool.

When I interviewed this manager, I expressed surprise that migration to the wiki was not faster and more spontaneous. I mentioned the extraordinary growth of Wikipedia and wondered aloud why his company hadn't experienced the same thing with its wiki. He explained that the comparison was invalid. Wikipedia, he said, can potentially draw on *all* Internet users as contributors. Even if only a tiny percentage of these potential contributors ever become actual contributors, this group will still be large enough to generate and refine Wikipedia's content.

A quick analysis showed that he was exactly right. In November 2005 (shortly after I did the interview) Wikipedia contained over 850,000 articles in English and 2.9 million across all languages. This content was generated by fewer than 50,000 contributors in English, 103,000 altogether. A *contributor* is defined by Wikipedia as someone with a user ID who's made at least ten total edits. Even this population is skewed: active English-language wikipedians (more than five contributions in a month) numbered 15,600 in that month, while very active (100 or more) numbered only 2,081.

The community of Wikipedia contributors is fairly large in absolute terms, but it's a tiny, almost negligible proportion of all English-speaking Internet users. When scaling down from the Internet to an intranet—in other words, when considering the use of an ESSP within an organization—if anything like the same percentage of users starts contributing, the platforms will remain almost totally empty, and the effort will be an abject failure.

It's easy to be impressed by the large, dynamic, and vibrant Web 2.0 communities on the Internet and to overlook the fact that they're actually quite tiny when expressed as a percentage of all Internet users. A key challenge, then, for all Enterprise 2.0 advocates is increasing the percentage of intranet users who contribute to their organizations' ESSPs.

To do this, it's critical to understand why the "ambient percentage" of contributors to organizational ESSPs isn't higher. Are the technologies themselves too primitive, or are they difficult to learn and use? Do some managers in an organization actually act to block Enterprise 2.0, because they don't want information to flow more freely? Or are the real roadblocks internal, rooted somewhere in the heads of individuals? Accurate answers to these questions are essential prerequisites to designing and executing successful efforts to deploy ESSPs.

In June 2008, at the Enterprise 2.0 conference, I moderated a panel of early adopters, including representatives from Wachovia Bank, Pfizer, Sony, and the IC. The first question I asked them, and the one on which we spent most of our time, was essentially, "If Enterprise 2.0 tools and approaches really are so beneficial and powerful, why haven't they spread like wildfire?" I suggested three categories of impediment: managers, technologies, and users, and invited the panelists to hold forth.

In their initial responses all of them identified users, not bad managers or inadequate technologies, as the biggest barriers to faster and deeper adoption of Enterprise 2.0. Entrenched practices and mind-sets and some degree of technophobia combine, they said, to limit the pace of adoption. These factors slow the migration from channels to platforms and necessitate continued patience, evangelism, and training.

I hadn't expected the panelists to say that the Enterprise 2.0 technologies themselves were so incomplete as to hinder adoption, but I was a bit surprised that in their first round of comments, none of them identified management as a real impediment. So I pressed the point by saying something like, "I didn't hear any of you point the finger at the managers in your organizations. Were you just being polite, or are they really not getting in the way of Enterprise 2.0? The new social software platforms are a bureaucrat's worst nightmare because they remove his ability to filter information, or control its flow. I'd expect, then, that each of you would have some examples of managers overtly or covertly trying to stop the spread and use of these tools. Are you telling me this hasn't happened?"

That is in fact what they were telling me, and I didn't get the impression that they were just being diplomatic. They said that managers were just another category of user that needed to migrate over to new ways of working, no more or less. In other words, the panelists hadn't observed managers in their organizations actively trying to impede Enterprise 2.0.

This surprised me. I'd assumed that since Enterprise 2.0 tools and approaches have no inherent respect for existing organizational hierarchies and boundaries, those who had ascended through the hierarchy and within the boundaries might be actively hostile to them. For the organizations represented on the panel, at least, that did not appear to be the case. The most counterproductive behaviors mentioned were the reflexive desire to work in private and the temptation to build a large number of mutually inaccessible ESSPs.

The panelists represented large organizations, most of which had been around for a long time and had large numbers of managers who were used to, and probably comfortable with, the status quo. Yet no examples surfaced of these managers trying to thwart or sabotage Enterprise 2.0 efforts, and no panelist told a story about managers darkly hinting to their groups that participating in these platforms might not be the best thing for a career. They talked instead about how hard it was to get people to change the way they worked, and to change the interaction and collaboration technologies they used.

Individual knowledge workers' failure to see the benefits of Enterprise 2.0 and adopt ESSPs can seem puzzling at first. After all, the new tools are both useful and easy to use. They require no advanced computer skills, offer novel capabilities, and benefit both organizations and people. They enable individuals to work more effectively with their strongly tied colleagues; build, maintain, and exploit a network of weak ties; and convert potential ties into actual ones. All of these activities also enhance the enterprise(s) where these individuals work. As Google's example shows, at least some people also derive value from trading in a prediction market, so the combination of individual- and group-level benefit persists even at the outermost ring of the Enterprise 2.0 bull's-eye.

It also seems as if enterprises should have little trouble increasing their "ambient percentage" of ESSP contributors to a level higher than that which exists on the Web. After all, organizations have a wide range of levers available to encourage desired behaviors. These levers include norms, incentives, objectives, policies, and whatever is meant by the important but vague notion of "corporate culture."

Organizations also usually have internal Enterprise 2.0 change agents and champions who are eager to both demonstrate the new ESSPs to their colleagues and to explain the advantages of using them. In many cases these evangelists will be younger employees and new entrants to the workforce, since members of Generation Y are much more likely than older workers to be comfortable with ESSPs—in fact, this group is sometimes called the "Facebook generation."

For all these reasons it seems that there should be relatively little persistent individual resistance to Enterprise 2.0, and that companies should quickly be able to turn their employees into competent and enthusiastic users of ESSPs. Yet this is not at all the situation that the panelists at the 2008 Enterprise 2.0 conference reported, and their experience appears to be typical. Many organizations, especially larger ones, have found that ESSPs remain a niche technology even well after their introduction, used by only a relatively small portion of the workforce, and lagging far behind the universal deployment of older channel technologies like e-mail. According to a global survey conducted by McKinsey, published in the *McKinsey Quarterly* in July 2008, only 21 percent of respondents expressed overall satisfaction with Web 2.0 tools, 22 percent expressed clear dissatisfaction, and 7 percent had tried at least one ESSP but had subsequently stopped using it.[9]

Of course many factors contribute to the comparatively slow spread of ESSPs among knowledge workers within enterprises. The explanation I have found most comprehensive and compelling comes not from research on information technology, but rather from investigations of why some consumer products fail to gain mass acceptance even though they are clearly "better mousetraps."

In a June 2006 *Harvard Business Review* article titled "Eager Sellers and Stony Buyers," Harvard Business School marketing professor John Gourville traced that phrase to a quote from Ralph Waldo Emerson: "If a man can write a better book, preach a better sermon, or make a better mousetrap than his neighbor, though he build his house in the woods, the world will make a beaten path to his door." Gourville concluded that this quote was compelling, but wrong; in fact, there are plenty of examples of products and services that offered clear advantages over those already in place—better mousetraps—yet never succeeded in replacing them.[10]

The stand-alone digital video recorder TiVo is one of the examples Gourville cites. TiVo drew rave reviews as soon as it was introduced in 1999, but the company had trouble generating sales sufficient to cover its heavy development and marketing expenses. By 2005 it had accumulated $600 million in operating losses.

TiVo's failure to gain mass acceptance quickly is especially puzzling, because it seems to be a clearly better mousetrap. When I speak to groups, I frequently ask TiVo owners to raise their hands. Fewer than one-third of the audience typically do so. I then ask these people to keep their hands in the air if they love their TiVo, if they can't imagine going back to the old, pre-TiVo way of watching television, and if they are essentially unpaid members of the TiVo sales force because they are always telling their friends how great the device is and encouraging them to purchase one. Most hands remain in the air throughout this sequence. I then ask in mock exasperation, "Why don't we all have a TiVo?"

Gourville drew on research in behavioral economics to answer this question. Among its many other accomplishments, this research has identified three consistent features of people's psychological "equipment" for making evaluations.

- *We make relative evaluations, not absolute ones.* When I'm at a poker table deciding whether to call a bet, I don't think of what my total net worth will be if I win the hand vs. if I lose it. Instead, I think in relative terms—whether I'll be "up" or "down."

- *Our reference point is the status quo.* My poker table comparisons are made with respect to where I am at that point in time. "If I win this hand I'll be up $40; if I lose it I'll be down $10 *compared with my current bankroll.*" It's only at the end of the night that my horizon broadens enough to see if I'm up or down for the whole game.

- *We are loss-averse.* A $50 loss looms larger than a $50 gain. Loss aversion is virtually universal across people and contexts and is not much affected by how much wealth one already has. Ample research has demonstrated that people find that a prospective loss of $x is about two to three times more painful than a prospective gain of $x is pleasurable.

When combined, these three elements lead to what the behavioral economist Richard Thaler has called the "endowment effect": we value items in our possession more highly than prospective items that could be in our possession, especially if the prospective item is a proposed substitute.[11] "We mentally compare having the prospective item to giving up what we already have (our "endowment"), but because we're loss-averse, giving up what we already have (our reference point) looms larger.

A related phenomenon is the "status quo" bias—our demonstrated preference for keeping what we already have even when equal or superior alternatives are available.

And Gourville points out three factors that make the situation worse for product developers who want their offerings to succeed. First is timing: adopters have to give up their endowment immediately, receiving benefits only sometime in the future. Second, these benefits are not certain; the new product might not work as promised. Third, benefits are usually qualitative, making them difficult to enumerate and compare.

As if all this weren't enough, Gourville also highlights the fact that the people who develop new products are generally quite dissimilar to the products' prospective consumers. You don't become a TiVo executive or engineer if you don't "get" the potential of digital video recorders and think they're a great idea. And after working for the company for a while, having TiVo becomes part of your endowment; you think of other new products in comparison to TiVo, instead of in comparison to a VCR or DVD. Both these factors make it harder for technology enthusiasts to see things as their target customers do.

All of these elements lead to what Gourville labels the "9X Effect"—a disparity of 9 to 1 between what innovators think consumers want and what consumers actually want. This effect goes a long way toward explaining the high-tech industry folk wisdom that to spread like wildfire, a new product has to offer a tenfold improvement over what's currently out there. For products that aren't inherently ten times better, Gourville offers important cautionary words:

> Many products fail because of a universal, but largely ignored, psychological bias: People irrationally

overvalue benefits they currently possess relative to those they don't. The bias leads consumers to value the advantages of products they own more than the benefits of new ones. It also leads executives to value the benefits of innovations they've developed over the advantages of incumbent products.

That leads to a clash in perspectives: Executives, who irrationally overvalue their innovations, must predict the buying behavior of consumers, who irrationally overvalue existing alternatives.

The results are often disastrous: Consumers reject new products that would make them better off, while executives are at a loss to anticipate failure. This double-edged bias is the curse of innovation.[12]

This curse, I believe, directly applies to enterprises as they attempt to deploy ESSPs and promote Enterprise 2.0. This is because acceptance of a new piece of technology among people who are free to use it or not is very much like consumer acceptance of any other new product. Therefore, the endowment effect and status quo biases apply.

E-mail is virtually everyone's current endowment of collaboration software. Gourville's research suggests that the average e-mail user will underweight the relative benefits of a replacement technology like an ESSP by about a factor of three, while Enterprise 2.0 enthusiasts will *overweight* these same benefits by the same factor (since for them ESSPs *are* the status quo). This is the 9X effect deployers of new collaboration technologies will have to overcome.

In most companies groupware and knowledge management (KM) systems didn't solve the problem, because they weren't *that* much better than e-mail. The current generation of Enterprise 2.0 tools is clearly different from groupware and KM and offers more and greater benefits. But that's not really the critical consideration. The critical consideration is brutally simple: are these tools nine times better than e-mail for collaboration?

Consider how high this sets the bar. E-mail is freeform, multimedia (especially with attachments), WYSIWYG, easy to learn and use, platform-independent, social, and friendly to mouse-clickers and keyboard-shortcutters alike. It would actually be a pretty tough competitor even if it *weren't* the universally used incumbent, and so the beneficiary of the 9X effect.

Within enterprises, where the incumbent collaboration technology of e-mail is well established, ESSPs are what Gourville calls "long hauls"—products that represent significant technological leaps forward and are therefore potentially quite valuable, but require major behavioral changes from their target audience. Long hauls have the potential to become popular and widespread, but their success comes slowly. Champions of long-haul products must be patient and prepared to evangelize, demonstrate, coach, train, and explain for what seems to them a very long time. As Gourville writes, "The simplest strategy for dealing with consumer resistance is to brace for slow adoption . . . to be successful companies must anticipate a long, drawn-out adoption process and manage it accordingly."[13]

7

Going Mainstream

A Road Map for Enterprise 2.0 Success

This chapter presents guidelines and advice to help leaders deploy the new social software tools successfully. It builds on the bull's-eye model and benefits described in chapter 4. Enterprise 2.0 success can't be reduced to a single step-by-step recipe; there are too many variables, and appropriate actions depend critically on both the goals of the effort and the characteristics of the organization. So this chapter presents a road map rather than a recipe; it stresses simple actions that leaders can take to increase the depth and breadth of their organizations' participation in the new digital environments.

Turning Off the Old

Gourville's research on the 9X effect and consumer adoption of novel products and technologies, discussed in chapter 6, suggests several strategies for overcoming resistance to Enterprise 2.0 and increasing adoption rates of emerging social software platforms (ESSPs).[1] One of these is simply to eliminate the old product and so force adoption of the new. At first this approach appears to be impracticable for ESSPs, because it would entail shutting down e-mail and the other incumbent channel technologies. Most companies are unwilling to do this, for good reason. Private communication channels are highly valuable, and it would be unwise to eliminate them completely just to force faster adoption of ESSPs.

For group-level work, however, the group's leader can come close to turning off e-mail by simply saying, "I'm not going to read e-mails about this project; put all updates on the wiki," or, "We're not going to write this report by e-mailing successive drafts of it around to each other; we're going to write it by making all of our edits to the single online version." At the innermost ring of the Enterprise 2.0 bull's-eye, where colleagues are strongly tied, managers can exercise a great deal of influence over the tools used for collaboration. In many instances they can eliminate the old channels completely and force migration to the new platforms.

It's also possible to eliminate existing methods at the second and third rings of the bull's-eye, where ties are weak or potential. As discussed above, few tools are currently in use at these two rings, and none of them works particularly well. Many organizations distribute digital or paper newsletters in an attempt to keep people updated on one another's activities, but it's probably safe to say that these are not the most eagerly consumed pieces of information. I often ask my students and audiences to raise their hands if they receive at least one "official" company newsletter; most hands go up. When I ask how many people routinely read them, very few hands remain in the air. These newsletters are filtered and edited sources of news, and they are forced on readers regardless of interest or demand.

An active enterprise blogosphere, on the other hand, is the product of many contributors, is not edited or filtered by any central authority, and is consumed primarily via search or signals such as really simple syndication (RSS). In a blogosphere readers decide what's relevant to them and then pull that content in, rather than relying on someone else to decide what information to push throughout the organization. Eliminating the old channels at the second and third rings of the bull's-eye simply means shutting down the existing set of newsletters and other "official" updates. I doubt they would be greatly missed.

Using Believers

For managers hoping to overcome the 9X effect with long-haul products, Gourville identifies believers as an important category of user. Believers are early and spontaneous adopters, who for some reason quickly see the benefits of the new product and switch to it. Managers can leverage Enterprise 2.0 believers by turning them into internal champions and evangelists. This strategy is particularly powerful if the believers are respected within the organization because of their rank, seniority, expertise, informal authority, and so on. The U.S. intelligence community (IC) is an example of an organization that is successfully employing this strategy. By the middle of 2008, Don Burke and Sean Dennehy at the CIA and Chris Rasmussen at the National Geospatial-Intelligence Agency were spending much of their time training, coaching, and encouraging their colleagues, both in person and online, about Enterprise 2.0.

Within most organizations the number of believers is bound to grow over time even without active evangelizing. This is because many, if not most, new entrants to the workforce are reflexive users of ESSPs, preferring platforms to channels for communication, collaboration, and interaction. A great deal of attention is currently being paid to Generation Y, the children of the baby boomers. This generation is also called "Millennials," because its members came of age—graduated from college and entered the workforce—after the year 2000. Many observers see significant differences between Millennials and previous generations, and it remains to be seen how many of these differences are significant and persistent.

It seems clear, however, that Generation Y uses technology almost intuitively, and uses different technologies than their elders do. In their book *Connecting to the Net.Generation: What Higher Education Professionals Need to Know About Today's Students*, Reynol Junco and Jeanna Mastrodicasa report that 75 percent of college students in the United States have a Facebook account and 28 percent author a blog.[2] Most Millennials, it seems safe to say, are believers in ESSPs and have an endowment of collaboration technologies that includes both channels and platforms.

These believers don't have rank, status, or authority within their organizations when they first enter the workforce, but they do have enthusiasm that can be harnessed. If enterprises choose not to recognize this and instead ignore Millennials' preference for ESSPs, they may not only be missing an opportunity but also are creating an unattractive work environment.

Most knowledge workers sit in front of computers for large portions of the day. The applications they use probably have a large impact not only on their productivity but also on their mood, as well as their affinity for the organization that put the tools in front of them. By 2008 I was starting to hear stories from managers about young employees who had left their organizations specifically because they were frustrated by the poor collaboration and knowledge-sharing tools available. An October 2006 survey in *The Economist* described how the global war for talent was heating up.[3] I imagine that an increasingly important front in that war, at least for new entrants to the skilled workforce, is going to be the technology environments that companies build and within which they expect their employees to do their work. Environments that support the way smart young people want to work, and are used to working, are going to look comparatively attractive.

Designing Technologies That Will Be Used

Technologists can mitigate the status quo bias by building ESSPs that work with existing communications tools like e-mail and text messaging rather than being direct substitutes for them. Many popular blog and wiki packages, for example, now allow users to send updates from e-mail accounts or mobile phones. Similarly, Facebook engineers have developed customized versions of their SNS for popular mobile devices, including Blackberries and iPhones.

Developers can further short-circuit the endowment effect and status quo bias by building applications for which no direct incumbent exists. As discussed above, Facebook became so popular so quickly in large part because it wasn't replacing anything—no widespread existing technology worked well for building, maintaining, and exploiting a network of weak ties. At the BBC, Euan Semple initiated Enterprise 2.0 with discussion forums because there was no online space where employees could pose a question to the entire organization in hopes that someone would have an answer for them.

Online forums have also become popular at many other companies—including Google, where Bo Cowgill used the corporate idea board to post his thoughts about a prediction market and find colleagues to help him build it. Of course, corporate prediction markets themselves are highly novel technologies. Before they existed, employees had no way to put their money where their mouths were regarding future events of interest to the company, or to convert their beliefs and hunches into a tradable portfolio.

Finally, technologists can reduce the amount of behavioral change required to use their products. Gourville divides successful products that aren't long hauls into two categories: easy sells and smash hits. McDonald's achieved an easy sell with an ESSP set up in advance of a 2007 franchisee conference. Attendees were asked in a preconference survey to describe any best practices they wanted to share with their peers. These were then collected and posted to the conference Web site, which was maintained by the ESSP vendor Awareness. Awareness built discussion forums around this set of practices so that franchise owners could interact with and learn from one another before, during, and after the conference. Rather than presenting the conference site to the franchisees as a potentially confusing wiki or blog, McDonald's and Awareness simply positioned it as a standard Web site with initial user-generated content and additional features. This was an easy sell.

Smash hits are innovations that "offer great benefits but require minimal behavioral change." The most recent Web 2.0 product to meet this definition is probably Twitter, the updating tool described in chapter 3. Twitter was started in late 2006, and by August 2008 it had approximately 2.4 million registered users and a volume of up-dates heavy enough to crash the entire service periodically and ne-cessitate a redesign of its architecture. Twitter lets people do something they couldn't do before—broadcast short updates on any topic of interest to the entire world and selectively consume others' updates—but it lets them do so using familiar tools and interfaces such as e-mail, mobile phone text messaging, and Web pages. By al-lowing users to carry out novel and valuable activities in deeply fa-miliar ways, Twitter became a smash hit.[4]

Six Organizational Strategies

It will, I hope, be clear by this point that the main challenges around Enterprise 2.0—the challenges of getting ESSPs widely and productively adopted within enterprises—are not the ones in-dicated by the questions listed in chapter 6, but instead those concerning people's choices, biases, and endowments. Enterprise 2.0 is ultimately the result of a large number of individual choices about which technologies to use for communication, collabora-tion, and interaction. If many people choose to use ESSPs, healthy and valuable online environments are likely to result. If, however, the great majority of people choose not to use ESSPs in their professional lives and instead to continue to communicate only via traditional channel technologies, their enterprises will not reap the benefits described in chapters 4 and 5.

Awareness of challenges leads to the development of effec-tive strategies for meeting them. My road map for success using Enterprise 2.0 has been developed through a combination of research, consulting, discussions with academics and practition-ers, observation, and awareness of existing relevant research in many fields. This road map has six main sections.

Determine Desired Results, Then Deploy Appropriate ESSPs

ESSPs all share some deep similarities, but they are emphatically not all identical. As case studies demonstrate, and as the examples in chapters 3 and 4 illustrate, ESSPs can produce many different outcomes for an organization. They can operate at different levels of tie strength, and they can deliver a range of benefits.

The first step in any Enterprise 2.0 effort should be the formation of a consensus about its goals. The conversation that yields this consensus should involve both business and IT leaders. The material presented in chapters 4 and 5 can, I hope, be of some value during this conversation, but the specific terminology and framework used during goal-setting discussions are not critical. What is critical is to arrive at a shared understanding of what the enterprise hopes to achieve. Is the main goal to enable strongly tied colleagues to do better group-level work? To let people broadcast their expertise, or their questions, throughout the organization? To build better weakly tied networks inside and outside the enterprise? To harness collective intelligence? As I hope this book has made clear, realizing each of these goals requires a different technology toolkit.

Each of the case studies in chapter 2 began with awareness of an open space—a need that was not being met or an opportunity that was not being seized. None of them began with a vague realization that something interesting was happening on the Internet with Web 2.0, or an equally hazy sense that it would be beneficial to do the same activities on the intranet. It's also the case that none of them began with a desire to bring "user-generated content" or "social media" into the organization. Rather, these ESSP deployments all started by identifying a fairly specific need or opportunity.

Being specific about needs and opportunities allows enterprises to be clear about which ESSPs they'll acquire. As these tools are being installed, the next step is for the organization to plan its adoption efforts.

Prepare for the Long Haul

As discussed earlier in this chapter, some ESSPs may be easy sells within organizations. If no incumbent technology is in place, and if no great behavioral changes are required, Enterprise 2.0 technologies can be quickly and widely adopted. Managers are often surprised to discover how many of their employees already have Facebook accounts, for example, and to learn that there is actually a formal Facebook network in place for their organization. Facebook spreads quickly in part because most people do not have a prior endowment of social networking software, and because it is easy and intuitive to use. And as previously noted, a technology like Twitter, which is highly innovative and delivers novel benefits without requiring individuals to make significant behavioral changes, may even be a smash hit within the enterprise.

Most of the tools of Enterprise 2.0, however, do require both behavioral and technological changes and are therefore long-haul products. Most of today's knowledge workers are not familiar with authoring for a broad audience, linking to and tagging online content, trading in a prediction market, or many of the other activities conducted on ESSPs. Furthermore, e-mail, at present the universally deployed collaboration technology, is part of the endowment and status quo for every worker. Because Enterprise 2.0 requires at least a partial shift away from this endowment, its adoption proceeds slowly—often more slowly than its enthusiasts expect.

Individuals, routines, processes, and organizations do not typically adapt quickly without a crisis or other forcing mechanism. Consequently, Enterprise 2.0 enthusiasts must learn patience and adjust their expectations to reflect the realities of a long-haul adoption.

The well-known examples of Web 2.0 successes—Facebook, Wikipedia, Delicious, Flickr, Twitter, and others—can convince observers that ESSPs are so inherently compelling that they essentially deploy themselves, becoming both broadly and deeply used with great speed. This perception, however, is inaccurate. As noted in chapter 6, only a very small percentage of Web users have ever actually contributed content to a Web 2.0 platform; if this same percentage were applied to the population of an enterprise, even a very large one, it would yield very few participants in Enterprise 2.0. Increasing the percentage of people within an organization who regularly contribute to ESSPs and ensuring that these platforms are healthy, vibrant, and sustainable environments is probably the work of years rather than months.

Communicate, Educate, and Evangelize

A critical component of this work, one that's probably at least as important as agreeing on the goals of the Enterprise 2.0 effort and selecting appropriate technologies, is communicating with the intended users of the new tools. This communication task can be divided into three phases: explaining to users the goals of the effort, training them on the tools themselves and related best practices, and continually encouraging them to contribute to ESSPs. The Serena and IC case studies are both examples of thorough communications programs. The IC's Intellipedians conduct frequent sabbatical programs in which analysts are taught both how to use tools like MediaWiki software and why they are valuable. After executives at Serena introduced the company's efforts to use Facebook extensively, they maintained their focus on these efforts over time through new initiatives such as using the SNS to plan and execute corporate social responsibility efforts.

Enterprise 2.0 enthusiasts are often surprised by how much effort is required to build and maintain momentum for their work, especially in the early phases of an adoption effort. But just as long-haul products typically require a great deal of marketing and advertising in the consumer world, so too do ESSPs require a sustained communications effort. In my experience many organizations underemphasize the first and last of the three phrases, instead focusing too heavily on training efforts. This attitude can leave a user community aware of how to contribute to the ESSPs but unsure why doing so would be a good thing.

Early adopters and Generation Y entrants into the workforce are typically the most enthusiastic trainers and evangelists for Enterprise 2.0, but the formal leaders of the organization must also participate actively in the communication effort. These leaders can send a credible signal that ESSPs are important, and that contributions to them will be valued. Senior executives at Serena were some of the earliest and most passionate advocates for using Facebook and other social software. Within the IC, top administrators have also been evangelists for Enterprise 2.0. As Michael Werthheimer, the assistant deputy director of national intelligence for analytic transformation and technology (who has been described as the "philosopher of transformation" for intelligence analysis), told the community of analysts in a major speech, "We are going to share more . . . We are going to take risks."[5]

Move ESSPs into the Flow

In a December 2007 post to his Transparent Office blog, Michael Idinopulos made an important distinction between using ESSPs "in the flow" of work—as part of the standard procedures for getting one's job done—versus "above the flow" of work—in addition to the standard activities of the workday. Concentrating on wikis, he wrote:

> Left to their own devices, people don't collaborate very much in above-the-flow ways. That was one of the great (if depressing) learnings of the Knowledge Management movement.
>
> Above-the-flow wikis are used lightly (when at all) by large groups of people. Many are encouraged to participate, but participating is rarely an urgent or critical-path activity. Lurking is extremely common, and the bulk of content comes from <5% of users who are either personally invested in the success of the project or just love to publish. Wikipedia works because of the law of large numbers: A small percentage of a huge number is still a large number.
>
> Adoption of in-the-flow wikis looks very different. It's not at all hard to get people to use in-the-flow wikis. They are used intensively by relatively small, well-defined groups of people: a project team, a business unit, etc. Once the group (or the group's manager) decides to use wikis as the primary collaboration tool, adoption is quite easy: People use it because that's the way to do their work. Lurkers are rare, since most people have a steady stream of things to contribute to the rest of the group.[6]

Idinopulos stressed that both types of ESSP have value, but cautioned that "[champions] should not expect an above-the-flow wiki like an internal knowledge exchange to have the same level of usage as an in-the-flow wiki."

From what I've seen, ESSPs that are perceived as being purely above the flow have difficulty sustaining momentum and often wither over time. For this reason champions of Enterprise 2.0 often work diligently to move ESSPs into the flow of their organization's work. Within the IC, for example, Don Burke and Sean Dennehy stress "Replace Existing Processes" as one of their three core principles of Enterprise 2.0 for intelligence analysis. At VistaPrint, Dan Barrett continually encouraged his colleagues to use the company's wiki instead of e-mail for sharing knowledge with one another. Over time, his persistence paid off, and the wiki moved into the flow of VistaPrint's knowledge work.

As these examples show, the decision to move ESSPs into the flow is often a deliberate one. Leaders can mandate that their teams will use group editing tools when writing a report, for example, or require that all departments, business units, and labs maintain blogs about their work. Some ESSP uses appear likely to remain above the flow—it's not obvious, for example, how trading in a prediction market can be moved into the flow—but in many, if not most, cases Enterprise 2.0 can become standard operating procedure.

Measure Progress, not ROI

It's possible to quantify many things about an Enterprise 2.0 initiative: the number of blog posts and comments; the number of wiki edits, editors, and new pages; the population of tags created; the volume of trades and traders in a prediction market; the number of members in a technology-facilitated social network and the volume of updates they share with one another; the popularity of all of these ESSPs as measured by the number of times they're viewed; and so on. Robust tools are available to collect and display all these types of data, and they serve as useful indicators of the progress and momentum of an adoption effort. Both Google and the IC have conducted extensive analyses of the activity on their ESSPs and use this information to both track and shape their initiatives.

It's also both possible and smart to collect case studies, anecdotes, and examples over the course of the effort to demonstrate the value of ESSPs. These examples serve two purposes. First, they illustrate desired actions and outcomes and so help to communicate the effort's goals to participants. Second, they help convince decision makers that the effort is yielding results and is thus worth continuing to fund and support.

I do not, however, advocate that decision makers should ask for quantitative ROI analyses, either before approving an Enterprise 2.0 effort or to assess its progress. This view may seem surprising, since most organizations have a long-standing tradition of using ROI figures to justify IT investments. So why should the new social software platforms be an exception to this tradition? Discussions about the ROI from Enterprise 2.0 always remind me of an experience I had during a seminar in 2006.

In this seminar I was presenting the concepts and structure of my MBA course to a diverse group of Harvard Business School colleagues. Pretty early on, one of the professors in the finance area asked me the question I was most dreading and least prepared for: "Andy, what do you teach students about conducting a financial analysis of a proposed IT investment?

How do you build a business case for IT?" I was about to launch into a long-winded and poorly argued answer, but Bob Kaplan spoke up first. "You can't," he said.

Kaplan is responsible for both activity-based costing and the balanced scorecard, so he speaks with no small authority on matters of costs and benefits. After the seminar he gave me a copy of *Strategy Maps*, which he wrote with David Norton. The subtitle of the book is *Converting Intangible Assets into Tangible Outcomes*. Intangible assets consist of human, organizational, and information capital; they define the latter as "databases, information systems, networks, and technology infrastructure."

The authors make their point forcefully and early in the book: "None of these intangible assets has value that can be measured separately or independently. The value of these intangible assets derives from their ability to help the organization implement its strategy. . . . Intangible assets such as knowledge and technology seldom have a direct impact on financial outcomes such as increased revenues, lowered costs, and higher profits. Improvements in intangible assets affect financial outcomes through chains of cause-and-effect relationships."[7]

This is a very crisp articulation of what I was going to try to say in the seminar. I've probably seen hundreds of business cases that identify the benefits of adopting one piece of IT or another, assign a dollar value to those benefits, and then ascribe that entire amount to the technology alone when calculating its ROI. The flaw in this reasoning is that the first two steps of this process are at best estimates, at worst pure speculation. The final step gives no credit and assigns no value to cotemporaneous individual- and organization-level changes. It's a little like giving all the credit for the Boston Red Sox 2004 World Series victory to manager Terry Francona, or hitter David Ortiz, or general manager Theo Epstein. Although all three were critical and probably even necessary elements, it would be ludicrous to say that any one of them was wholly responsible for the win.

Usually, even the most rigorous and objective IT business cases are exercises in speculation and attribution. And most IT business cases are something less than rigorous and objective. At their worst, they are like Soviet five-year plans—devices used by competing groups to come up with ever-bigger numbers in order to secure funding and avoid hard scrutiny.

IT is vexing because its costs are so clear, and often so high. Indeed, on paper concrete expenses make IT look like a new machine tool, assembly line, or factory, none of which a responsible company would buy without first conducting financial analyses. The difference between IT and these other fixed assets is that machine tools and factories add value directly, not through "chains of cause-and-effect relationships."

A company invests in a new assembly line because it needs greater widget capacity. If it had that increased capacity, it could make and sell more widgets. The relationship between costs and financial benefits in this case is complicated in some ways (depending on many factors, some of which must be estimated), but the cause-and-effect chain is a short one, and one that *doesn't* depend on lots of cotemporaneous changes.

With IT, in contrast, cause-and-effect chains are often quite long and dependent on changes in human and organizational capital, as well as information capital. It wasn't enough, for example, for IntraWest just to purchase and install an ESSP that included blogging capability. Employees had to become comfortable contributing to this new social platform, searching for and consuming its information, and using it as a tool for collaborating with their remote colleagues.

IT looks very much like a standard capital investment—a company pays cash and acquires an asset, whether that asset is a server or a CD full of software, the right to access a system over a network, or any other innovation. But this money-for-assets exchange represents only surface-level activity. The real phenomenon of interest is the attempt to acquire an IT-based benefit, just as advertising is an attempt to build a brand and R&D is an attempt to innovate. Each of these attempts requires sustained management attention, not just a periodic contest among business cases in which the highest ROI figure wins.

So does this mean that companies should just stop building business cases for Enterprise 2.0 initiatives and other IT efforts, and proceed instead solely by intuition or the persuasiveness of a sales pitch? Of course not. I counsel Enterprise 2.0 advocates to put together a business case that has three main elements:

- *Costs and time lines:* The cost portion of the cost-benefit analysis can and should be calculated with all due precision. The cost breakdowns of most types of IT effort are well understood by now and should be laid out in advance. So should the best initial guesses about how long the whole effort will take, how it will be segmented, and what milestones will be reached along the way. When doing this, it's important and smart to acknowledge the great uncertainty inherent in both anticipating costs and timing, especially for large and complex projects.

- *Benefits expected:* The previous section categorizes the benefits that ESSPs can deliver. While these benefits are not as low-level as the feature sets of any particular piece of software, neither are they as high-level as some of the promised results from IT like "organizational transformation" and "customer intimacy." They provide a foundation for a concrete discussion of outcomes from Enterprise 2.0 that doesn't rely on knowledge of any specific vendor's offerings. When describing benefits, it's often useful to include short case studies or examples of the results of other ESSP deployments. One such case study could be, "At Intrawest blogging allowed a cost savings of $500,000 to be transmitted throughout the company, and management believes that the transmission would not have occurred without the blogging platform." Examples like these show decision makers that Enterprise 2.0 does yield impressive results.

- *Technology footprint:* A technology's footprint is its geographic, divisional, and/or functional reach. It's a description of how much territory a piece of IT is intended to cover. Some information technologies such as e-mail have large footprints that are easy to expand. Others have fairly small ones; a computer-aided design system isn't that useful outside the engineering department. For ESSPs, the footprint is closely related to the concept of tie strength. Social software platforms that are intended to span the outer rings of the bull's-eye—where ties are weak, potential, or nonexistent—must have much larger footprints than those that span only strongly tied colleagues. As previously discussed, most of the benefits of Enterprise 2.0 increase as the technologies span more types of ties and so have larger footprints.

Cost, capability, and footprint in most cases constitute sufficient information to allow business leaders to make IT decisions.

They also provide a basis for prioritizing IT initiatives, something many companies struggle with. Is it more important for customer interaction processes to be standardized across all business units, or for vendor interaction processes to be? Is it more important to change how engineers collaborate, or to give them better tools for experimentation? These are not easy questions, but they are important and appropriate for leadership to discuss.

The comparison of dollars spent in relation to benefits acquired isn't one that yields an ROI number, but it's one that business leaders are adept at making. Most of the executive teams I've worked with would have little trouble answering questions like, "Is it worth spending $1 million and tying up the following resources for the next six months in order to build a broadcast search system that will span weak and potential ties?" I don't mean to imply that the answer to such questions is always yes. I simply mean that most business leaders can answer them quickly because they're posed in familiar terms—as cost-versus-benefit trade-offs.

Across the hundreds of quantitative IT business cases I've seen, I'd estimate the average ROI figure at about 100 percent. This observation raises a couple of obvious questions, which I have asked every business case author I could find: "If this ROI figure is at all accurate, *why are companies spending money on anything else except IT?* If there really are all these 100 percent ROI projects out there, doesn't Finance 101 say that companies should immediately start lots of them and not stop until the marginal return is less than the return from traditional investments such as advertising, R&D, capacity expansion, and so on?"

I never got a satisfactory answer to this question until I read *Strategy Maps* and saw Kaplan and Norton's points about how nebulous the numerator—the financial returns—of this ROI figure is, and how the denominator actually comprises not only IT capital but also human and organizational capital.

Walking away from ROI-based business cases for Enterprise 2.0 efforts does *not* mean walking away from careful thinking or analytical rigor, nor does it mean abandoning any important management duties. Rather, it entails acknowledging that IT is a lot more like R&D than like a new machine tool, and that reliance on large ROI numbers is both a shortcut and a potentially dangerous habit.

In my experience, ROI calculations for IT efforts more often than not wind up being exercises in justifying what someone already knows he wants to do. I am convinced that decision makers are easily capable of comparing the costs of an Enterprise 2.0 effort against the benefits it will provide, even if the two elements of this comparison are not expressed in identical financial terms. Chapters 4 and 5 can help Enterprise 2.0 advocates articulate the benefits of ESSPs, and it's straightforward to calculate the costs of a deployment. A discussion of whether it's worthwhile to pursue Enterprise 2.0 should revolve around whether these benefits are worth the cost, not whether the ROI figure for the project clears some hurdle rate. I have never spoken with a leader or participant in a healthy Enterprise 2.0 initiative who wishes that she had calculated an ROI figure, whereas I have spoken with many people who have described their ROI exercises as unproductive uses of time and effort.

Show That Enterprise 2.0 Is Valued

Perhaps the most frequently asked question I've heard related to the adoption of ESSPs is, "What incentives should we put in place to best encourage participation and contribution?" This is clearly a critical question, since incentives strongly influence behavior. As they begin to investigate social software, enterprises often ask themselves what new incentives, if any, to offer, and how, if at all, to modify existing ones.

Across organizations that have experience with Enterprise 2.0 there is a rich mix of beliefs and viewpoints about proper incentives. Some believe in relatively concrete and obvious signs of recognition and appreciation for good contributors. Within the IC, for example, particularly active Intellipedia editors were sent a small plastic shovel with the words "I dig Intellipedia! It's wiki wiki, Baby" on the handle and, more recently, a coffee mug with the words "Intellipedia: it's what we know." In addition to these small gifts, it was also customary to send the editor's supervisor a letter describing the contributions and expressing gratitude. Google distributed both cash prizes and T-shirts to the company's most active traders and other star performers in the internal prediction market (the T-shirts turned out to be more highly valued). These concrete symbols provide gratification and an ego boost to ESSP contributors, as well as serving to start subsequent conversations about Enterprise 2.0.

Other organizations advocate making contributions to ESSPs part of an employee's formal objectives or job description. This approach reflects a belief that making Enterprise 2.0 "part of everyone's job" is the best way to accelerate it. Organizations that adopt this attitude hope that the relatively hard incentive will encourage even older and less tech-friendly workers to investigate the new tools and eventually incorporate them into their work. This approach is particularly common among enterprises seeking the benefit of authoring; they want people to commit their expertise in digital form to an ESSP like a blog, wiki, or answer board.

Organizations put incentives in place to encourage behaviors that they desire or value. This reality points to a single broad and powerful guideline for fostering Enterprise 2.0 that goes beyond the specifics of any incentive plan: *demonstrate that contributions to ESSPs are valued.* Perhaps the most straightforward way in which the leaders of an organization can do this is to consult and use these contributions themselves. Commenting on blogs, asking the authors of wiki pages questions, and bringing up content from an ESSP during a meeting are examples of quick and simple, yet effective, ways of showing that the new platforms, their content, and their participants are all important. My experience, observations, and intuition indicate that activities like these by managers and executives may well be the most powerful ways of fostering Enterprise 2.0.

8

Looking Ahead

The Vision, the Liar's Club, and Model 1 Versus

Model 2 Behavior

T his concluding chapter looks into the future of Enterprise 2.0. It begins by presenting a vision of an organization that has fully deployed emergent social software platforms (ESSPs) and goes on to discuss what I believe will be the two biggest obstacles to achieving this vision. The first is the simple fact that not everyone within an organization wants information to flow and grow more freely. The second, and more troubling, is the well-documented finding that even organizations that sincerely want to change and become more open and transparent often have great difficulty doing so.

This chapter reveals the reasons for these barriers and ends on a hopeful note by stressing that while entrenched organizational practices can make Enterprise 2.0 difficult, the tools and approaches of Enterprise 2.0 can themselves be very powerful weapons for changing these practices. It ends by returning to the question posed in the introduction: *does IT matter* in competitive battles? Does it differentiate organizations from each other and help separate winners from losers? I'll wrap up this book by presenting an argument in favor of why technology matters and showing how Enterprise 2.0 increases its importance.

The case studies presented at the start of this book and the ensuing discussion of the unique benefits available from ESSPs suggest a vision of an organization that has fully embraced Enterprise 2.0. This organization's digital environments—its intranet, extranet, externally facing Web site, and so on—are much more open and dynamic than they used to be. The organization itself is more multivoiced; people have ample opportunity to express themselves, to share their knowledge, and to be helpful to colleagues no matter how remote or weakly tied they are. Within this enterprise redundancy is low, questions are answered quickly and accurately, and people aren't continually "reinventing the wheel." More improvements, innovations, and other good ideas are surfaced and the best of these rise to the top and become prominent. Expertise is easy to locate, and people are better able to stay in touch with large numbers of current, past, and potential colleagues. People build and maintain larger weakly tied networks and can call on these networks for help, advice, and information. Many different kinds of digitally mediated conversations take place, ranging from long, dense, and detailed to short and bursty.

This organization uses the wisdom of crowds to help answer important questions about future events, and it also lets the crowd determine what's important, high quality, or otherwise noteworthy. Customers, suppliers, and other external parties can participate in many ESSPs. People feel more connected to one another because they *are* more connected, and as a result they also feel a tighter bond with the organization as a whole.

It's important to stress that this idealized organization is not exactly like an ant colony—a completely self-directed entity. As this book has hopefully made clear, Enterprise 2.0 is not incompatible with leadership, management, and hierarchy. I believe, in fact, that leadership and management are essential for the successful deployment of ESSPs and that emergent digital environments can coexist quite peacefully with established hierarchies. Enterprise 2.0 is not a substitute for formal organization, in other words, but rather a highly valuable complement to it.

If an organization can overcome the 9X effect and successfully introduce the long-haul products of Enterprise 2.0 so that they are both widely and deeply adopted throughout the target population of users, then what? Will the vision described above be realized and maintained over time? After all, there are no technological barriers to achieving it, and the business needs it addresses are certainly real. So once many people start using the new ESSPs, can anything stop them?

On the Internet, the answer appears to be no. It is difficult to imagine that Web 2.0 will be shut off or reversed, or that it will fade because people grow tire of contributing content. Whether or not any of the currently popular Web 2.0 communities continue to grow and thrive, the trend toward participation in ESSPs is an enduring one. The Internet is no longer primarily a resource where content is created by a few and passively consumed by many. Instead, much of its most popular content is both created and consumed by large numbers of people, and millions of individuals shift easily between the roles of creator, consumer, and community member. Will this fluidity also inevitably be the case for most organizations?

I don't believe that it will, for two main reasons. The first, and more obvious, is that not everyone wants information and knowledge to flow more freely within an organization. This reluctance has nothing to do with security concerns; it occurs because some information makes some parts of an organization look bad, and the people involved will therefore want to keep this information from becoming widely known. I noted in chapter 6 that the panelists at the 2008 Enterprise 2.0 conference had not yet observed managers trying to impede or shut down ESSP deployments. I imagine, however, that this situation will change over time, at least in some organizations.

The Liar's Club and Enterprise 2.0

Hiding or covering up unfavorable information within organizations is nothing new; there are countless examples of such behavior. My favorite is contained in an article by David Ford of Texas A&M and John Sterman of MIT, "The Liar's Club: Concealing Rework in Product Development."[1] According to the authors:

> Concealment is often standard practice. At a major defense contractor, weekly meetings of project team leaders were known as "the liar's club" because everyone withheld knowledge that their subsystem was behind schedule. Members of the liar's club hoped someone else would be forced to admit problems first, forcing the schedule to slip and letting them escape responsibility for their own tardiness. Everyone in the liar's club

knew that everyone was concealing rework require-
ments and everyone knew that those best able to hide
their problems could escape responsibility for the project failing to meet its targets.

I highlight the liar's club because it is precisely the kind of
information hiding that becomes much more difficult with
Enterprise 2.0. Imagine that an organization with a liar's club
seeks the benefit of authoring, giving all employees the ability
to blog and to comment on others' blogs. And imagine further
that at least some of this authoring can be done anonymously.
It seems very likely that at least some of the people frustrated
by the liar's club, perhaps the engineers on the projects, will
use the authoring platforms to expose and discuss the constant
concealment.

Another possibility is that the organization could pursue
the Enterprise 2.0 benefit of collective intelligence and so deploy prediction markets on the intranet. It would then be easy
to set up markets around questions like, "Will subsystem x be
completed on time?" If organizational prediction markets are in
fact as accurate and decisive as they appear to be, they will
quickly yield clear answers about which subsystems, if any,
won't be completed on time. Even though the ESSPs deployed
in these two scenarios are dissimilar, the results are the same: the
revelation of information runs counter to the liar's club, and
threatens it.

What will be the final result in this situation? Will the liar's
club evaporate, or will the ESSPs be shut down? The answer de-
pends heavily on the goals and attitudes of the most senior people within the organization. If they want the truth to be known,
there are excellent tools available for revealing it. But these

tools will bring with them some level of dissent and disagree-ment. They will make some people uncomfortable and cast oth-ers in a poor light. In many cases these people will be relatively senior and influential within the organization, and they will be adamant that the new tools are not working well—that they're inaccurate, spreading rumors rather than the truth, or encourag-ing people to waste time rather than do their work.

Sorting out these claims, and deciding how to proceed in the wake of the discomfort caused by Enterprise 2.0, is the re-sponsibility of senior executives, not lower-level managers or IT department employees. The actions and responses of these ex-ecutives will be closely watched. If they appear to side with the liar's club, enthusiasm for Enterprise 2.0 could quickly fade. If, on the other hand, they show support for authoring, collective intelligence, and the other benefits available from ESSPs, enthusiasm is more likely to persist and grow.

Enterprise 2.0 and the Shift from Model 1 to Model 2

The second longer-term threat to Enterprise 2.0, and in many ways the deeper one, comes not from managers who don't want more truth and franker discussion within their organizations, but rather from those who sincerely do. The work of Chris Argyris, an emeritus professor at Harvard, has shed much light on how this paradoxical result can occur.

Over a distinguished career, Argyris studied why it is so dif-ficult for most organizations to learn, change, and improve themselves, even when the need for change is broadly acknowl-edged and the desire for improvement is real and widespread. In a series of detailed long-term studies he demonstrated that even with the best of intentions, organizations and the people within them fall into traps that keep them locked in unproductive patterns of behavior and interaction. The truly vexing aspect of these traps is that they spring not from the urge to be selfish or deceitful—as in the case of the liar's club—but instead from the desire to be a good person and colleague, one who is interested in both improving the organization and taking care of the people within it.

To understand Argyris's traps, it is first necessary to understand what he describes as "Model 1" behavior by people and organizations (see table 8-1). Model 1 is a theory-in-use rather than an espoused theory; in other words, it's what people actually do, regardless of what they say they are doing. Argyris and his colleagues have articulated both the governing values of Model 1 and some of the action strategies (in other words, activities) that derive from these values.

TABLE 8-1

Model 1 theory of behavior

Governing variables	Action strategies
Define goals and try to achieve them.	Design and manage the environment unilaterally (be persuasive, appeal to larger goals, etc.).
Maximize winning and minimize losing.	Own and control the task (claim ownership of the task, be guardian of the definition and execution of the task).
Minimize generating or expressing negative feelings.	Unilaterally protect yourself.
Be rational.	Unilaterally protect others from being hurt.

Source: Chris Argyris and Donald A. Schön, *Organizational Learning II: Theory, Method, and Practice* (Reading, MA: Addison-Wesley, 1996), 68–69.

At first glance, none of this looks bad or harmful. Model 1's governing values, in particular, seem productive for both individuals and organizations. Who could argue with rationality, goal setting, a desire to win, or an unwillingness to generate negative feelings? Argyris's great contribution has been to show that they in fact lead to highly counterproductive behaviors that limit the ability to change and improve. As he and David Schön wrote in their 1996 book *Organizational Learning II: Theory, Method, and Practice*, "To the extent that one behaves according to any of the four action strategies, one will tend to behave unilaterally toward others and protectively toward oneself. If successful, such behavior controls others and prevents one from being influenced by them. But as a consequence, the actor tends to be seen as defensive (since he or she is defending), and interpersonal and intergroup relations tend to become more defensive than facilitative, more a matter of win/lose than of collaboration. These effects tend to generate mistrust and rigidity."[2]

A more complete and less favorable list of Model 1's action strategies and their consequences is shown in table 8-2.

Argyris and Schön go on to note:

Given these governing variables and strategies, there is likely to be little public testing of the assumptions embedded in theories-in-use, because such testing would require confronting one's own defensiveness and the defensiveness of others . . .

In our earlier book *Theory in Practice* . . . we describe the resulting situation as follows:

. . . lack of such public testing risks creating self-sealing processes . . . the individual . . . cuts himself

TABLE 8-2

Consequences of Model 1 behavior

Governing values	Action strategies
Define goals and try to achieve them.	Design and manage the environment unilaterally (be persuasive, appeal to larger goals, etc.).
Maximize winning and minimize losing.	Own and control the task (claim ownership of the task, be guardian of the definition and execution of the task).
Minimize generating or expressing negative feelings.	Unilaterally protect yourself (speak in inferred categories accompanied by little or no directly observable data, be blind to impact on others and to incongruity; use defensive actions such as blaming, stereotyping, suppressing feelings, intellectualizing).
Be rational.	Unilaterally protect others from being hurt (withhold information, create rules to censor information and behavior, hold private meetings).

Source: Chris Argyris and Donald A. Schön, *Organizational Learning II: Theory, Method, and Practice* (Reading, MA: Addison-Wesley, 1996), 68–69.

off from the possibility of disconfirming assumptions about his theory-in-use and . . . his starting
assumptions . . .

The actor needs minimally distorted feedback from
others. If others provide such feedback—especially if they
do so with some risk—and if they experience that the
actor is not open to change, they may believe that they
have placed themselves in a difficult situation. Their mistrust of the actor will probably increase, but this fact will
be suppressed. The result will be the creation of another
series of self-sealing processes that again make the actor
less likely to receive valid information . . .[3]

Argyris summarizes the unhappy final result of this dynamic, and of the "defensive reasoning" that underlies Model 1:

> Model I tells individuals to use action strategies where they craft their positions, their evaluations, and their attributions in ways that inhibit inquiries into and tests of them. The result is escalating errors, self-fulfilling prophecies, and self-sealing processes . . . But, what if the intended consequences are . . . openness, transparency, and trust? These cannot be produced by miscommunication, escalating errors, self-fulfilling prophecies, and self sealing processes. [When the intended consequences are openness, transparency, and trust] the user of Model I . . . is faced with a dilemma. He uses Model I strategies to achieve consequences that will not be produced by Model I theory-in-use.
>
> The logic [of Model 1] is (1) send a message that is inconsistent, (2) act as if it is not inconsistent, (3) make steps 1 and 2 undiscussable and make undiscussability undiscussable.[4]

I find this to be a very tidy summary of the dysfunctions I have observed within many organizations.

If people and organizations want to break out of this pattern of defensiveness, cover-up, and "undiscussability," Argyris recommends that they abandon the governing values of Model 1 and replace them with the Model 2 governing values and associated action strategies shown in table 8-3.

As Argyris and Schön explain, the governing values and action strategies of Model 2, which can be summarized as

TABLE 8-3

Model 2 theory of behavior

Governing values	Action strategies
Valid information	Design situations where participants can be origins of action and experience high personal causation.
Free and informed choice	Jointly control task.
Internal commitment to the choice and constant monitoring of its implementation	Protect self as a joint enterprise, and be oriented toward growth.
	Bilaterally protect others.

Source: Chris Argyris and Donald A. Schön, *Organizational Learning II: Theory, Method, and Practice* (Reading, MA: Addison-Wesley, 1996), 87.

"productive reasoning" rather than defensive reasoning, are not opposite to those of Model 1:

> Model 2 does not reject the skill or competence to advocate one's purposes. It does reject the unilateral control that usually accompanies advocacy because the typical purpose of advocacy [in Model 1] is to win. Model 2 couples articulateness and advocacy with an invitation to others to confront the views and emotions of self and other. It seeks to alter views in order to base them on the most complete and valid information possible and to construct the positions to which people involved can become internally committed . . .
>
> The behavioral strategies of Model 2 involve power sharing with anyone who has the competence and is relevant to deciding about implementing the action in question . . . *Individuals in a Model 2 world seek to find the*

people most competent for the decision to be made or the problem to be solved. They seek to build viable decision-making networks in which the major function of the group is to maximize the contributions of each member so that when a synthesis is developed, it incorporates exploration of the widest possible range of views (emphasis added).[5]

I am deeply interested in Enterprise 2.0 not because its component technologies are novel, innovative, and powerful (although they are) and not because I believe that ESSPs will fundamentally transform how enterprises are designed, rendering hierarchy obsolete (I do not believe this will be the case). I'm most interested in the use of ESSPs because they can help organizations move from a Model 1 to a Model 2 theory-in-use. These tools can change the nature of collaboration and discussion within an enterprise, giving people the ability both to contribute their perspective to a dialogue and to inform themselves by incorporating multiple perspectives. In short, they can help organizations move from defensive to productive reasoning.

The move from Model 1 to Model 2 entails giving up unilateral control over both the goals *and* the tasks used to accomplish these goals. In Model 2 unilateral control is replaced with decision making based on valid information, an emphasis on "winning" is replaced with free and informed choice, and defensiveness is replaced with constant monitoring of choices made. ESSPs can be tremendously valuable in accomplishing each of these transitions.

As has been explained throughout this book, the new social software platforms are inherently multivoiced and egalitarian. They also facilitate emergence—the appearance of patterns and structure over time as a result of many low-level, autonomous activities and interactions. Emergence means that ESSPs are easy to search and navigate; people can find whatever information they're looking for as they strive to make informed choices, and they no longer have to rely only on official information.

It is critical to stress that Enterprise 2.0 alone will not move people and organizations from Model 1 to Model 2 theories-in-use. Argyris and his colleagues have shown that sustained interventions are required during which people are first made to see that they are perpetuating Model 1 (despite their sincere belief that they are doing no such thing) and then shown how to recraft their interactions to lead to Model 2. Even the best of the new social software platforms are no substitute for these interventions, but they can be effective complements to them.

At its core, Enterprise 2.0 is about giving many more people within the organization a voice, letting them interact as equals, and harvesting what emerges. Like Model 2, Enterprise 2.0 is about abandoning the assumption that unilateral control is the best way to achieve desired outcomes, and instead trusting in people's ability to interact productively without constant supervision from above. Both Model 2 and Enterprise 2.0 are hostile to the idea that the "undiscussable" should remain taboo—that the liar's club or any other ongoing charade within an organization should persist.

Enterprise 2.0 enthusiasts would do well to learn from Argyris and his colleagues, who have clearly noted the difficulties and long time lines involved in moving from Model 1 to Model 2 and shown the relatively low awareness of Model 2. Argyris often states that it takes as long to become proficient in productive reasoning and Model 2 interactions—which are more evidence-based, less unilateral, less defensive, *and* less likely to provoke defensiveness in others—as it does to learn to play a decent game of tennis or golf. And this estimate presumes that the involved parties all *want* to move to Model 2, which in many organizations is far from a sure bet.

As I consider the state of knowledge about Enterprise 2.0 at the time of writing (spring 2009), I feel very much the same. We have the examples of some leading organizations in this area that are willing to share their experiences, insights, and lessons learned. We also have a large amount of relevant research from disciplines as diverse as sociology, computer science, consumer behavior, and organizational psychology. This research suggests both how organizations can benefit from Enterprise 2.0 and how they can accomplish the transition to broad and deep use of ESSPs. In this book I have attempted to bring these case studies and prior research together with my own work on the topic and present what I believe is a convincing rationale for pursuing Enterprise 2.0, as well as useful guidance about how to do so.

Managers, executives, and organizations looking only for certainty or the "one best way" will likely come away disappointed by this book, and probably unenthusiastic about Enterprise 2.0 in general. The use of ESSPs will instead resonate with people and organizations seeking a conversation rather than a speech, who agree with the British political philosopher Michael Oakeshott that "[c]onversation is not . . . a contest where a winner gets a prize, . . . it is an endless, unrehearsed, intellectual adventure in which in imagination we enter a variety of modes of understanding the world and ourselves. And, we are not disconcerted by the differences, or dismayed by the inconclusiveness of it all."[6]

There are new technologies available to support and sustain this conversation, and ample reason to believe that it will leave organizations better off. It is up to the leaders of an enterprise to decide if they want to open themselves up to the conversation.

The Importance of Technology

My deepest professional conviction is that IT *matters*—that it affects both performance and competition, increasing differences between companies and separating winners from losers. I arrived at this belief through working from the bottom up, writing cases and conducting research on individual companies, and then trying to assemble the resulting mass of anecdotes, observations, examples, and case studies into coherent patterns.

As I documented runaway IT successes, painful failures, and everything in between, I thought and wrote about their broader implications. I also read and taught IT-related materials that my colleagues had developed and folded them into the pattern recognition work. Finally, I undertook a fair amount of executive education and consulting and as a result saw firsthand how a broad range of companies and managers approach technology issues.

The most striking and consistent pattern I observed was large differences, or spread, in how companies approach IT—in their willingness to invest, in the types of technology they select, in how they manage and lead during adoption efforts, and most of all in the benefits they receive, even if they select identical technologies. My work, in short, led me away from the view that IT is irrelevant to competition—that it's the great equalizer or competitive leveler—and toward a very different conclusion—that technology is a profound competitive differentiator.

This conclusion, however, was based on pattern matching across a small set of examples. Other people could, and did, look at other examples and reach different conclusions about IT's impact. The best known of these, of course, was Nicholas Carr's 2003 contention in *Harvard Business Review* that "IT

Doesn't Matter."[7] The debate that followed the appearance of Carr's article highlighted the need to move beyond collecting case studies and examples one at a time, and instead carry out more comprehensive and systematic research on IT's competitive impact.

In the summer of 2008 *Harvard Business Review* published "Investing in the IT That Makes a Competitive Difference," an article I wrote with Erik Brynjolfsson.[8] We presented the results of research we conducted with Feng Zhu and Michael Sorell to examine IT's influence on competition over time in every U.S. industry, using data on the performance of every publicly traded company.

There were two striking trends in the mass of data we collected and analyzed. First, competition started to heat up in the United States in the mid-1990s, just as the Web and large-scale commercial enterprise systems began to be widely and deeply used by businesses. As a group, U.S. industries started to become more concentrated—more dominated by a few large firms—at this time. They also became much more turbulent—the ranking of companies in terms of sales and market value started to vary a lot more from year to year. And the spread in performance among competitors in an industry—the difference between high and low performers in measures such as gross profit margin, return on assets, and market capitalization per dollar of revenue—started to increase. In short, competition became nastier, a broad finding that affirmed the patterns I saw in my case writing and field research.

The second clear trend was that all of these competitive changes were significantly more pronounced in industries that invested heavily in IT. The more technology an industry absorbed, in general, the more competition intensified from the mid-1990s on. In summary, our analyses showed a clear association between IT intensity and competitive intensity, and between IT intensity and performance spread.

In our article we laid out our theory explaining why IT is not coincidental to these competitive changes, but is instead driving them. We argued that IT, especially the types of corporate technology that have been available since the mid-1990s, is a uniquely powerful tool for leveraging good business ideas and for propagating them widely and with high fidelity.

As discussed in chapter 1, until recently most types of enterprise software, including ERP, CRM, and SCM, have leveraged good ideas by imposing them. These technologies first predefine workflows, interdependencies, decision rights, and acceptable types of information; they then deploy these rules and ensure that they are followed.

I have argued in this book that the great promise of Enterprise 2.0, in contrast, is that it allows good new business ideas to emerge from anywhere and spread organically, rather than being developed at the center and imposed from the top down. As this book's examples and arguments illustrate, the use of ESSPs does not typically lead to chaos, decreased effectiveness, or greater risk. Instead, when properly deployed, these technologies yield highly useful digital collaboration environments that are easy to search and navigate, capture and spread knowledge, provide high-quality answers to important questions, and increase both the number and strength of ties among people.

By accomplishing these tasks, Enterprise 2.0 increases the number of good ideas that an organization develops and delivers to its consituencies. Some of these ideas—for example, a better process for taking and filling customer orders—can be incorporated into an ERP system and so disseminated throughout a company. Others can be directly integrated into products. Still others can spark a productive conversation or meeting or put hours back into the week of a busy knowledge worker.

The ESSPs themselves are largely indifferent to these different types of ideas; the new collaborative tools of Web 2.0 and Enterprise 2.0 simply provide forums in which people come together with few preconditions or constraints and generate remarkably powerful content and ideas.

Good ideas are the lifeblood of virtually every business. Unless you own a diamond mine, oil well, or patent on the wheel, you cannot afford to be complacent or to let your business model become stale. Our research strongly indicates that in recent years IT has served to raise the premium on good new business ideas.

I am confident that Enterprise 2.0 is going to increase this premium even more and further separate winners from losers in the competitive battles to come. My experience has led me, and this book has hopefully led you, to two conclusions: that ESSPs are very powerful tools, and that not all organizations will deploy and use them with the same skill and enthusiasm. Some will be discouraged by the apparent risks and threats, others will be unenthusiastic about possible benefits, and many will simply remain unaware of ESSPs and what they can accomplish. In addition, as chapters 6 and 7 discuss, not all companies that pursue Enterprise 2.0 will be successful. ESSPs are long hauls, requiring a great deal of attention, leadership, and patience. Not all organizations will have enough of these resources to succeed.

As a result of all these factors, Enterprise 2.0 and the new tools of collaboration and interaction will help perpetuate the trend we've observed recently of increased spread and larger performance differences across companies. Rather than causing companies to become more similar to one another, they'll produce the opposite effect and accentuate their differences. Some competitors will use the new tools to let more good ideas emerge and so increase both the stock and flow of beneficial innovations; others will not. Over time the companies with more good ideas will pull away from the pack.

I'm aware that these are fairly bold and sweeping claims. But all of my work has shown me that they are accurate ones. I hope this book has shown you something of the power of Enterprise 2.0, interested you in the possibilities offered by the new technologies of collaboration, and encouraged you to make use of them. Good luck!

Notes

Chapter 1

1. http://www.wired.com/wired/archive/7.04/blackout_pr.html.

2. http://en.wikipedia.org/w/index.php?title=Skinhead&oldid=10892675.

3. Nicholas G. Carr, "IT Doesn't Matter," *Harvard Business Review*, May 2006, 41-49; Nicholas G. Carr, *Does IT Matter? Information Technology and the Corrosion of Competitive Advantage* (Boston: Harvard Business School Press, 2004).

4. Andrew P. McAfee, "Enterprise 2.0: The Dawn of Emergent Collaboration," *Sloan Management Review*, April 2006, 21-28.

Chapter 2

1. Dan Barrett, interview by author, September 2008.

2. Chicago Crime eventually became part of the Web site everyblock.com.

3. Kyle Arteaga, interview by author, July 2008.

4. Thomas H. Kean and Lee H. Hamilton, *The 9/11 Commission Report: Final Report of the National Commission on Terrorist Attacks Upon the United States* (New York: W.W. Norton, 2004). Tenet's quote appears on page 259; the title of the August 6, 2001, president's daily brief is given on page 260.

5. In addition to the report of the 9/11 Commission itself, Lawrence Wright's *The Looming Tower* (New York: Alfred A. Knopf, 2006) is an excellent source of information on bin Laden, those in America who perceived his threat, and information-sharing failures within and among the agencies responsible for preventing terrorist attacks.

6. http://archives.cnn.com/2002/US/05/21/phoenix.memo/index.html.

7. Wright, The *Looming Tower,* 389.

8. http://www.time.com/time/covers/1101020603/memo.html.

9. Kean and Hamilton, *The 9/11 Commission Report,* 268–272; also Wright, *The Looming Tower.*

10. Kean and Hamilton, *The 9/11 Commission Report,* 272.

11. Ibid., 416–418.

12. Ibid., 418–419.

13. http://www.docstoc.com/docs/886365/DNI-ANNUAL-REPORT-TO-CONGRESS.

14. http://www.globalsecurity.org/intell/library/reports/2005/wmd_report_25mar2005_overview.htm.

15. http://www.slate.com/id/2110767/.

16. James Surowiecki, *The Wisdom of Crowds: Why the Many Are Smarter Than the Few and How Collective Wisdom Shapes Business, Economies, Societies, and Nations* (New York: Doubleday, 2004).

17. Joyce E. Berg, Robert Forsythe, Forrest D. Nelson, and Thomas A. Rietz, "Results from a Dozen Years of Election Futures Markets Research" (forthcoming in C.A. Plott and V. Smith, eds., *Handbook of Experimental Economic Results*), http://www.biz.uiowa.edu/iem/archive/BFNR_2000.pdf.

18. The accuracy of the Hollywood Stock Exchange was highlighted in Justin Wolfers and Eric Zitzewitz, "Prediction Markets," *Journal of Economic Perspectives* 18, no. 2 (Spring 2004): 107–126, http://bpp.wharton.upenn.edu/jwolfers/Papers/Predictionmarkets.pdf.

19. http://www.arthurdevany.com/2007/02/seeing_things_a.html.

20. Surowiecki, *The Wisdom of Crowds.*

21. Peter A. Coles, Karim R. Lakhani, and Andrew P. McAfee, "Prediction Markets at Google," Harvard Business School Case no. 9-607-088 (Boston: Harvard Business School Press, 2007).

22. Ibid.

23. N. Chauhan and N. Bontis, "Organisational Learning via Groupware: A Path to Discovery or Disaster?" *International Journal of Technology Management* 27, no. 6 (2004): 591–610.

24. Thomas H. Davenport, *Thinking for a Living: How to Get Better Performance and Results from Knowledge Workers* (Boston: Harvard Business School Press, 2005).

Chapter 3

1. http://www.oreillynet.com/pub/a/oreilly/tim/news/2005/09/30/what-is-web-20.html.

2. Delicious was originally known as Del.icio.us.

3. http://radar.oreilly.com/archives/2006/12/web-20-compact-definition-tryi.html.

4. Paul Dourish, "Process Descriptions as Organisational Accounting Devices: The Dual Use of Workflow Technologies" (proceedings of the 2001 International ACM SIGGROUP Conference on Supporting Group Work), 52–60.

5. http://mail.wikimedia.org/pipermail/wikien-l/2003-February/001149.html.

6. http://en.wikipedia.org/wiki/Nupedia.

7. Ibid.

8. "Wikipedia (A)," Harvard Business School online case, http://courseware.hbs.edu/public/cases/wikipedia/.

9. Marshall Poe, "The Hive," *Atlantic Monthly*, September 2006, http://www.theatlantic.com/doc/200609/wikipedia.

10. Delicious Web site.

11. http://archive.salon.com/21st/rose/1998/12/21straight.html.

12. http://blog.searchenginewatch.com/blog/060629-105413.

13. This is Wikipedia's definition of social software.

14. http://www.artima.com/intv/wiki.html.

15. Meredith Morris, *How Do Users Feel About Technology?* Forrester Research Report, http://www.forrester.com/Research/Document/Excerpt/0,7211,35895,00.html.

16. http://archive.fosdem.org/2005/index/interviews/interviews_wales.html.

17. http://www.forbes.com/best/2004/1213/bow001.html.

18. http://en.wikipedia.org/wiki/Five_pillars_of_Wikipedia.

19. http://blogs.nature.com/wp/nascent/2005/12/comparing_wikipedia_and_britan_1.html.

20. http://en.wikipedia.org/wiki/Wikipedia:External_peer_review/Nature_December_2005/Errors.

Chapter 4

1. Richard Gillespie, *Manufacturing Knowledge: A History of the Hawthorne Experiments* (Cambridge, UK: Cambridge University Press, 1991) is perhaps the best summary of the Hawthorne experiments and the massive amount of discussion, research, and debate that they initiated.

2. Mark Granovetter, "The Strength of Weak Ties: A Network Theory Revisited," *Sociological Theory* 1, no. 1 (1983): 201–233.

3. Ibid.

4. Morton T. Hansen, "The Search-Transfer Problem: The Role of Weak Ties in Sharing Knowledge Across Organization Subunits," *Administrative Science Quarterly* 44, no. 1 (1999): 82–85. Morton Hansen, Marie Louise Mors, et al., "Knowledge Sharing in Organizations: Multiple

Networks, Multiple Phases," *Academy of Management Journal* 48, no. 5 (2005): 776-793. Daniel Levin and Rob Cross, "The Strength of Weak Ties You Can Trust: The Mediating Role of Trust in Effective Knowledge Transfer," *Management Science* 50, no. 11 (2004): 1477-1490.

5. Granovetter, "The Strength of Weak Ties."

6. Ronald Burt, *Structural Holes* (Cambridge, MA: Harvard University Press, 1992), 17-18.

7. Dan Barrett, interview by author, September 2008.

8. Kyle Arteaga, interview by author, July 2008.

9. Dunbar's papers on the "Dunbar number" include Robin Dunbar, "Neocortex Size as a Constraint on Group Size in Primates," *Journal of Human Evolution* 20 (1992): 469-493; and Robin Dunbar "Co-Evolution of Neocortex Size, Group Size and Language in Humans," *Behavioral and Brain Sciences* 16, no. 4 (1993): 681-735. Dunbar also wrote a popular book about his work: Robin Dunbar, *Grooming, Gossip, and the Evolution of Language* (Cambridge, MA: Harvard University Press, 1996).

10. http://online.wsj.com/article/SB119518271549595364.html?mod=googlenews_wsj.

11. https://www.cia.gov/library/center-for-the-study-of-intelligence/csi-publications/csi-studies/studies/vol49no3/html_files/Wik_and_%20Blog_7.htm.

12. https://www.cia.gov/library/center-for-the-study-of-intelligence/csi-publications/csi-studies/studies/vol49no3/html_files/Intelligence_Networking_6.htm.

13. Clive Thompson, "Open Source Spying," *New York Times Magazine*, December 3, 2006.

14. https://www.intelink.gov/wiki/Three_Core_Principles, accessed May 20, 2009.

15. Nancy M. Dixon and Laura A. McNamara, "Our Experience with Intellipedia: An Ethnographic Study at the Defense Intelligence Agency," February 5, 2008, https://cfwebprod.sandia.gov/cfdocs/CCIM/docs/DixonMcNamara.pdf.

16. http://www.fastforwardblog.com/2007/01/08/survey-proves-90-of-managers-are-clueless/.

17. http://www.urbandictionary.com/define.php?term=meatspace.

18. Peter A. Coles, Karim R. Lakhani, and Andrew P. McAfee, "Prediction Markets at Google," Harvard Business School Case no. 9-607-088 (Boston: Harvard Business School Press, 2007).

19. Ibid.

20. Friedrich Hayek, "The Use of Knowledge in Society," *American Economic Review* 35, no. 4 (1945): 519-530.

21. Tim Harford, *The Undercover Economist: Exposing Why the Rich Are Rich, the Poor Are Poor—and Why You Can Never Buy a Decent Used Car!* (New York: Oxford University Press, 2006).

Chapter 5

1. A summary of Wenger's work can be found at http://www.ewenger.com/theory/.

2. Daniel G. Bobrow and Jack Whalen, "Community Knowledge Sharing in Practice: The Eureka Story," *Reflections* 4, no. 2 (2002): 47–59.

3. *Democratizing Innovation* is available online at http://web.mit.edu/evhippel/www/democ1.htm.

4. http://www.socialtext.net/cases2/index.cgi?intrawest_wiki_intranet.

5. Dava Sobel, *Longitude: The True Story of a Lone Genius Who Solved the Greatest Scientific Problem of His Time* (Toronto: Penguin, 1996).

6. Karim Lakhani, Lars Po Jeppesen, Peter Lohse, and Jill Panetta, *The Value of Openness in Scientific Problem Solving* (Boston: Harvard Business School Publishing, 2007).

Chapter 6

1. http://en.wikipedia.org/wiki/Internet_troll.

2. http://www.webopedia.com/TERM/F/flame_war.html.

3. https://ttlc.intuit.com/app/full_page. For a review, see http://review.zdnet.com/accounting-finance/intuit-turbotax-2007-premier/4505-6405_16-32850170.html, which contains the following: "TurboTax includes a new peer-support system, called Live Community, which lets users post and answer questions. This is an improvement upon prior versions because it lets users answer each other's odd questions, such as how a pet breeder should treat the death of animals in their care. The crowd's contributions to Live Community also bubble time-sensitive details to the surface, such as updates about the alternative minimum tax."

4. http://www.e-consultancy.com/news-blog/364781/bazaarvoice-ceo-brett-hurt-on-customer-reviews.html.

5. http://blogs.zdnet.com/social/?p=439.

6. JP Rangaswami, interview by author. Rangaswami was one of the first executives outside the high-tech industry to blog; he maintains the excellent Confused of Calcutta blog at http://confusedofcalcutta.com/.

7. On Spitzer's prosecutions of the analysts Jack Grubman, Henry Blodgett, and others, see Charles Gasparino, *Blood on the Street: The Sensational Inside Story of How Wall Street Analysts Duped a Generation of Investors* (New York: Free Press, 2005). On the porousness of Chinese walls, see, for example, Hasan Nejat Seyhun, "Insider Trading and the Effectiveness of Chinese Walls in Securities Firms," *Journal of Law, Economics and Policy*: 1001 (forthcoming).

8. JP Rangaswami, interview by author, July 2008.

9. http://www.mckinseyquarterly.com/Information_Technology/Management/Building_the_Web_20_Enterprise_McKinsey_Global_Survey_2174.

10. John T. Gourville, "Eager Sellers and Stony Buyers: Understanding the Psychology of New-Product Adoption," *Harvard Business Review,* June 2006, 98–106.

11. Richard Thaler, "Toward a Positive Theory of Consumer Choice," *Journal of Economic Behavior & Organization* 1, no. 1 (March 1980): 39–60.

12. John T. Gourville, "Why Consumers Don't Buy: The Psychology of New Product Adoption." Harvard Business School Note #504–056 (Boston: Harvard Business School Publishing, 2004).

13. Ibid.

Chapter 7

1. John T. Gourville, "Why Consumers Don't Buy: The Psychology of New Product Adoption." Harvard Business School Note #504–056 (Boston: Harvard Business School Publishing, 2004).

2. Reynol Junco and Jeanna Mastrodicasa, *Connecting to the Net.Generation: What Higher Education Professionals Need to Know About Today's Students* (Washington, DC: NASPA, 2007).

3. Robert Last, "The War for Talent Is NOT a Myth," *The Economist,* October 5, 2006, 1–2.

4. "Home Tweet Home," *Sloan Management Review,* July–August 2008, user account information from www.twitdir.com.

5. http://www.govexec.com/dailyfed/0907/092407nj1.htm.

6. http://michaeli.typepad.com/my_weblog/2007/12/in-the-flow-and.html.

7. Robert S. Kaplan and David P. Norton, *Strategy Maps: Converting Intangible Assets into Tangible Outcomes* (Boston: Harvard Business School Press, 2004).

Chapter 8

1. David N. Ford and John D. Sterman, "The Liar's Club: Concealing Rework in Concurrent Development," *Concurrent Engineering: Research and Applications* 11, no. 3 (2003): 211–219.

2. Chris Argyris and Donald A. Schön, *Organizational Learning II* (Reading, MA: Addison-Wesley, 1996).

3. Ibid., 95.

4. Ibid., 78.

5. Ibid., 117–119.

6. Michael Oakeshott, *The Voice of Liberal Learning: Michael Oakeshott on Education,* ed. TimothyFuller (New Haven: Yale University Press, 1989).

7. Nicholas G. Carr, "IT Doesn't Matter," *Harvard Business Review,* May 2006, 41–49.

8. Andrew McAfee and Erik Brynjolfsson, "Investing in the IT That Makes a Competitive Difference," *Harvard Business Review,* July–August, 2008.

Index

adoption of E2.0
  challenge of increasing the
    percentage of users, 163
  concerns about participation,
    146-148
  consumers and the endowment
    effect and, 168-169
  e-mail as a competitor,
    170-171
  evaluation methods used by
    consumers, 168-169
  example of benefits of E2.0
    to a company, 155-157
  factors contributing to slow
    adoption, 166-167
  factors favoring adoption
    of ESSPs, 165-166
  factors hindering product
    developers, 169
  hesitancy of users seen as an
    impediment, 164
  keeping behavioral change
    required minimal, 177-179
  lack of reported negative
    outcomes, 148

legal risks to allowing unmoni-
    tored Intranet discussions,
    157-159
  managers' acceptance of
    ESSPs, 165
  9X Effect and, 169-170
  open platform benefits for
    regulated industries, 158-160
  organizational strategies for
    (see organizational strategies
    for adopting E2.0)
  percentage of potential contribu-
    tors who become actual
    contributors, 162-163
  risk of embarrassing information,
    154-155
  risk of inaccurate information,
    153-154
  risk of inappropriate behavior
    and content (see risks
    of E2.0)
  risks of information theft, 159-161
al-Mihdar, Khalid, 32
Amazon, 72, 139
Andrus, Calvin, 104-105, 107

Argyris, Chris, 200–204, 207
Arteaga, Kyle, 29, 98, 100, 102
authoring using ESSPs, 71,
    133–136
automated tie suggesters, 91
Awareness (ESSP vendor), 178

Barrett, Dan, 26, 92, 185
BBC, 112–114, 137, 177
behavior models. *See* patterns of
    behavior and interaction in
    companies
benefits of ESSPs
    authoring, 71, 133–136
    broadcast search, 136–137
    collective intelligence, 139–140
    group editing, 130–133
    impact on ties between people
        (*see* tie strength)
    network formation and
        maintenance, 137–139
    non-exclusive value of all
        attributes, 141–142
    self-organization, 140–141
    value from bringing people
        into contact, 138
Bialik, Carl, 103
blogosphere, 175
blogs
    ability to convert potential ties
        into actual ties, 111–112
    origins of, 49
    potential to have prevented 9/11,
        106–107
    value of authoring, 133
Bonvanie, René, 97
Brin, Sergey, 64–65
broadcast search, 136–137
Brynjolfsson, Erik, 210
bull's-eye rings, 86–88, 125–127.
    See also tie strength
Burke, Don, 108, 114, 175, 185
Burt, Ronald, 85

Burton, Jeremy, 27, 97
Burton, Michael, 106

Carr, Nicholas, 11, 209
case studies. *See* prediction market
    at Google; Serena Software;
    U.S. Intelligence Community;
    VistaPrint
Clarke, Richard, 30, 31
collective intelligence, 139–140
communities of practice, 131–132
computer-supported collaborative
    work (CSCW), 39
Connecting to the Net.Generation (Junco
    and Mastrodicasa), 176
content risks from unmonitored
    contributions. *See* risks
    of E2.0
Cowgill, Bo, 36, 38, 117–118,
    121–122, 137
Cross, Rob, 84
Cunningham, Ward, 57, 71
customer relationship management
    (CRM), 53

Davenport, Thomas, 40–41
Delicious, 58, 60–62, 67–69, 71
Deming, W. Edwards, 54
Democratizing Innovation
    (von Hippel), 132
Dennehy, Sean, 107, 175, 185
de Vany, Arthur, 37
Diggs, 139
Directorate of National
    Intelligence (DNI), 160
directories, 90
document repositories, 90–91
Dougherty, Dale, 44
Dourish, Paul, 53
Dresnder Kleinwort Wasserstein
    (DrKW), 157, 158
Dunbar, Robin, 102, 103

E2.0 *See* Enterprise 2.0
"Eager Sellers and Stony
    Buyers" (Gourville), 167
e-mail, 41, 47, 170-171
emergence, phenomenon of, 67
emergent social software platforms.
    See ESSPs
Encyclopedia Britannica, 78-79
endowment effect and consumers,
    168-169
Enterprise 2.0 (E2.0)
    ability to counteract the liar's
        club, 198-200
    adopting (*see* adoption of E2.0)
    bull's-eye ring model of, 86-88,
        125-127
    component technologies
        of, 195
    definition and use as a
        tool, 73-74
    promise of, 211-213
    new platforms used by (*see*
        ESSPs)
    opportunities available from (*see*
        benefits of ESSPs)
    as a tool to move from defensive
        to productive reasoning,
        206-207
    vision of an organization that has
        fully embraced, 196-197
enterprise resource planning
    (ERP), 53
ESSPs (emergent social software
    platforms)
    adoption of (*see* adoption of
        E2.0)
    benefits of using (*see* benefits of
        ESSPs)
    company examples of embracing
        (*see* prediction market at
        Google; Serena Software; U.S.
        Intelligence Community;
        VistaPrint)

contribution to a company (*see*
    ROI from E2.0)
defined, 69-73
inappropriate use of (*see* risks
    of E2.0)
limits to fluidity of
    intraorganizational, 198
related positions on the bull's-eye
    rings, 127
tie strength concept and (*see* tie
    strength)
Eureka system from Xerox, 132
extensions as an ESSP
    feature, 72

Facebook, 138, 181
Facebook use at Serena
    addressing questions about
        privacy and appropriateness
        of entries, 99-100
    attributes making it appropriate
        for weakly tied collaborators,
        101-102
    benefits arising from use of,
        100-101, 104
    contribution to goal of learning
        about Web 2.0, 99
    efforts to introduce and educate
        employees on its use, 97-98
    levels of participation, 100
    most commonly used
        feature, 98
    qualities that made its use
        attractive, 97
    social network building
        advantages, 102
FBI, 31
flame wars, 151
Flickr, 69, 71
folksonomy, 68, 72
Ford, David, 198
free and easy platforms, 49

Galileo Awards, 35, 104-105
Generation Y, 166, 176-177
Goldman, Willliam, 37
Google
    creation of a prediction market
        (*see* prediction market at
        Google)
    PageRank algorithm, 65-66
Google Docs, 92
Gourville, John, 167, 168, 169,
    171, 178
Granovetter, Mark, 82, 83
group editing, 130-133
groupware, 40, 53

Hannay, Timo, 78-79
Hansen, Morton, 84
Harford, Tim, 125
Hartigan, Mike, 135
Hawthorne effect studies, 82
Hayek, Friedrich, 123
Hazmi, Nawaf al-, 32
Hollywood Stock Exchange,
    37, 118, 126

IC. *See* U.S. Intelligence
    Community
ICES (Intelligence Community
    Enterprise Services), 107-108
Idinopulos, Michael, 184
IEM (Iowa Electronic Markets), 36,
    118, 126
inappropriate use of ESSPs. *See*
    risks of E2.0
Innocentive, 136-137
instant messaging (IM), 41, 47
Intelligence Community Enterprise
    Services (ICES), 107-108
Intelligence Reform and Terrorism
    Prevention Act of 2004, 34
Intellipedia, 108-109, 160
intranets, 42

Intrawest Placemaking, 134
"Investing in the IT That Makes
    a Competitive Difference"
    (McAfee and Brynjolfsson), 210
Iowa Electronic Markets (IEM), 36,
    118, 126
IT (information technology)
    association with competitive
        intensity and performance
        spread, 211
    commoditization of, 11-12
    communications technologies
        actually used, 41-42
    Enterprise 2.0 and (*see* Enterprise
        2.0)
    group-level technology available
        in 1980s-1990s, 40
    influence on competition in U.S.
        industries, 210
    middle managers' discomfort
        with, 9-11
    recent important new technolo-
        gies, 4
    role as a competitive differentia-
        tor, 209
    sustained benefit of, 3-4
    tech sector's tendency towards
        hype, 4-6
    Web 2.0 and (*see* Web 2.0)
"IT Doesn't Matter" (Carr), 11,
    209-210

Jeppesen, Lars Po, 137
Junco, Reynol, 176
Juran, Joseph, 54

Kaplan, Robert, 187, 191
Kaplan, Fred, 35
Kirnos, Ilya, 38-39, 118
knowledge management (KM)
    systems, 40, 41, 53
Kovitz, Ben, 57

Lakhani, Karim, 137
Levin, Daniel, 84
liar's club, 198–200
Liebling, A. J., 48
LinkedIn, 101
links as an ESSP feature, 70–71
Linnaeus, Carl, 59
Lohse, Peter, 137
Lotus Notes, 40
Lovas, Bjorn, 84

managers and executives
    ability to dissuade inappropriate
        behavior, 150–152
    choice of adopting E2.0
        technologies, 208
    general acceptance of ESSPs, 165
    influence on participation in
        E2.0, 194, 200
    discomfort with IT, 9–11
    use of "believers" to draw others
        in, 175
"mashups," 28
Mastrodicacsa, Jeanna, 176
Mayo, Elton, 82
McAfee, Andrew, 210
McConnell, J. Michael, 34
McGrath, Chris, 134
meatspace, 114
MediaWiki, 92, 95, 96
Millennials. *See* Generation Y
mobile phone texting, 47
Model 1 and Model 2 theory of
    behavior. *See* patterns of
    behavior and interaction
    in companies
Mors, Marie Louise, 84
Moussaoui, Zacarias, 31

National Commission on Terrorist
    Attacks Upon the United
    States, 30, 33–34

Nature, 78
network formation and mainte-
    nance, 137–139
9/11 Commission, 30, 33–34
9X Effect, 169–170
Norton, David, 187, 191
Nupedia, 55–57

Oakeshott, Michael, 208
O'Neill, Paul, 30
OpenRoad Communications, 134
O'Reilly, Tim, 44, 45
*Organizational Learning II: Theory,
    Method, and Practice* (Argyris and
    Schön), 202
organizational strategies for
    adopting E2.0
    communicating, educating,
        evangelizing, 182–183
    determining desired results,
        180–181
    measuring progress, not ROI (*see*
        ROI from E2.0)
    moving ESSPs into the flow,
        184–185
    preparing for slow-paced
        adoption, 181–182
    showing that contributions are
        valued, 192–194

Page, Larry, 65
PageRank algorithm, 65, 69
Panetta, Jill, 137
participation in E2.0
    concerns about, 146–148
    incentives that encourage,
        192–194
    increasing at the company level,
        174–175
    increasing at the group level, 174
    keeping required behavioral
        change minimal, 177–179

participation in E2.0 (*continued*)
  leveraging Generation Y's
    affinity for ESSPs, 176-177
  possible employee retention
    advantage from adoption, 177
  using "believers" to draw others
    in, 175
patterns of behavior and interaction
  in companies
  challenge in moving from Model
    1 to Model 2, 207-208
  Model 1 and defensive
    reasoning, 204
  Model 1 consequences, 202-204
  Model 1 theory of behavior,
    201-202, 207
  Model 2 and productive
    reasoning, 204-206
  Model 2 theory of behavior,
    204-206, 207
  tool to move from defensive to
    productive reasoning, 206-207
Paulos, John Allen, 63-65
Pender, Robert, 98
permalinking, 111
platforms. *See* ESSPs; Web 2.0
  platforms
Policy Analysis Market, 118
potential ties. *See also* tie strength
  converting potential ties into
    actual ones in the IC (*see* U.S.
    Intelligence Community)
  difficulty of converting potential
    ties to actual ties, 89-90
  potential ties turned into actual
    ties at Google, 119-120
  SNS's ability to facilitate weak
    and potential ties, 97
prediction market at Google
  ability to generate information
    from untied people, 122-125
  accuracy of, 121-122
  Cowgill's interest in starting,
    117-118, 137

Cowgill's interest in *Wisdom of
    Crowds,* 36
information-generating
  properties, 123-124
launch of, 120-121
message board used to
  introduce the idea,
  118-119
potential ties turned into actual
  ties turned into project work,
  119-120
prediction markets
  creation at Google (*see* prediction
    market at Google)
  described, 36-38
  harnessing of collective
    intelligence, 139
  potential to counteract the liar's
    club, 199
  similarity to linking and tagging,
    126-127

Rangaswami, JP, 157, 158-159
Rasmussen, Chris, 175
Raymond, Eric, 16
risks of E2.0
  attribution as a mitigator,
    149-150
  concerns about, 149
  counterbalance of informal and
    formal leaders, 150-152
  self-policing as a limiting
    factor, 150
  sense of what is appropriate as a
    mitigator, 152-153
  ways to guard against, 153
ROI from IT
  average ROI figure for IT,
    191, 192
  business case for E2.0 adoption,
    189-190, 192
  collection of supportive
    anecdotal evidence, 186

comparison of dollars spent in
relation to benefits required,
191, 192
complexity of quantifying
benefits of IT, 188–189
folly of seeking quantitative ROI
analysis of progress, 186–187
inability to decouple IT from
cotemporaneous changes,
187–188
types of data available for
ESSPs, 186
Rosenberg, Scott, 65, 66
RSS, 73

Salon.com, 64–65
Sanger, Larry, 55
Scheuer, Michael, 30
Schön, David, 202–204
SCM (supply chain
management), 53
search as an ESSP feature, 70–71
self-organization through
ESSPs, 140–141
Semple, Euan, 112–114, 137, 177
Serena Software
business background, 27
concern about lack of ties
between employees, 84–85
desire to increase sense of
community, 29
engagement in continuing
education in SNS uses,
182–183
planned move into
"mashups," 28
SNS use to build corporate
culture (*see* Facebook use at
Serena)
SharePoint, 96
signals as an ESSP feature, 72–73
simultaneous editing, 92
skinheads and Wikipedia, 1, 3, 7–9

SLATES (*s*earch, *l*inks, *a*uthoring,
*t*agging, *e*xtensions, *s*ignals),
70–73
Sloan Management Review, 12
social networking software
(SNS)
ability to facilitate weak and
potential ties, 97
blurring of border between
personal and professional
lives, 104
emergent platforms (*see* ESSPs)
Facebook's use by a company (*see*
Facebook use at Serena)
need for continuing education in
uses, 182–183
research on number of people
possible in a social network,
102–103
Sorell, Michael, 210
Sterman, John, 198
Strategy Maps (Kaplan and Norton),
187, 191
"Strength of Weak Ties, The"
(Granovetter), 82–84
strong ties, 82–84, 91–92. *See also* tie
strength
Structural Holes (Burt), 85
StumbleUpon, 72
supply chain management
(SCM), 53
Surowiecki, James, 36, 38

tag clouds, 67–68
tags, 60–62, 68, 71–72
taxonomies, 59, 68
Taylor, Frederick Winslow, 54
Tenet, George, 30
Thaler, Richard, 168
theories of behavior. *See* patterns of
behavior and interaction in
companies
Thompson, Clive, 106

ThoughtFarmer, 134-135
tie strength
  benefits of having a densely inter-
    linked Intranet, 112-114
  blurring of border between
    personal and professional
    lives, 104
  challenges of version control and
    simultaneous editing, 92
  defined, 81-82
  currently used technologies for
    exploiting weak ties, 88-89
  difficulty of converting potential
    ties to actual ties, 89-90
  ESSPs' ability to convert poten-
    tial ties into actual ties, 114-117
  example of converting potential
    ties into actual ties (*see* U.S.
    Intelligence Community)
  Facebook used to create ties (*see*
    Facebook use at Serena)
  fourth ring on the bull's-eye,
    125-127
  information lost when structural
    holes are unspanned, 87
  problems with strong-ties
    technology, 91-92
  researchers' tendency to focus
    on small groups of close
    colleagues, 82
  research on number of people
    possible in a social network,
    102-103
  SWT applied to companies, 84-85
  technological tools aimed at
    potential ties, 90-91
  tie circles of the prototypical
    knowledge worker, 86-88,
    125-127
  unspanned structural holes and,
    85-86
  untied people connected through
    prediction markets (*see* predic-
    tion market at Google)

VistaPrint's use of wikis, 93-96
  weak ties versus strong ties roles,
    82-84
TiVo, 167, 169
trolls, 149
Twitter, 50, 178, 181

Undercover Economist, The
  (Harford), 125
"Use of Knowledge in Society,
  The" (Hayek), 123
U.S. Intelligence Community (IC)
  addressing the risk in informa-
    tion sharing, 160-161
  advocacy of wiki use, 107-108
  blog use, 111-112
  bringing ESSPs into the
    flow, 185
  consequences of lack of effective
    information sharing, 31-33
  core principles of ESSPs use in
    IC, 109-110
  cultural barrier to change, 35
  engagement in continuing educa-
    tion in SNS uses, 182-183
  ESSPs ability to convert
    potential ties into actual
    ties, 104-106, 114-117
  greatest value derived from
    ESSPs, 114
  how ESSPs could have prevented
    9/11, 106-107
  Intellipedia development and
    launch, 108-109
  need for a shift in philosophy and
    policy, 34-35
  9/11 Commission recommenda-
    tions, 33-34
  possession of an intranet environ-
    ment suited to ESSPs, 107
  potential of wikis and blogs, 105
  prevalence of unspanned struc-
    tural holes throughout, 85-86

scattered warning signs of a probable attack, 30-31
successful adoption of internal wiki, 110-111
use of "believers" to draw others in, 175
USS *Cole*, 32

Vander Wal, Thomas, 68
Varian, Hal, 120
version control, 92
VistaPrint
  business model, 23-25
  information-sharing challenges due to rapid growth, 25-27
  switch from e-mail to wiki use, 185
  up-selling strategy, 24
  wiki employed to capture and spread knowledge, 92-94
  wiki's ease and efficiency of use, 94-96
von Hippel, Eric, 132

Wales, Jimmy, 55, 74-75
weak ties. *See also* tie strength
  currently used technologies for exploiting, 88-89
  Facebook attributes making it appropriate for weakly tied collaborators, 101-102
  SNS's ability to facilitate weak and potential ties, 97
  versus strong ties, 82-84
Web 2.0
  concept and definition of, 44
  Enterprise 2.0 and (*see* Enterprise 2.0)
  lack of imposed structure (*see* Web 2.0 structure)
  market trading's similarity to linking and tagging, 126-127

  mechanisms for emerging structure (*see* Web 2.0 structure)
  network effects and, 46
  platforms for communication and interaction (*see* Web 2.0 platforms)
  skepticism about, 6
  SNS use to facilitate weak and potential ties, 97
  Wikipedia and, 6-9 (*see also* Wikipedia)
Web 2.0 platforms
  assumption that platform use is difficult, 51
  channels for private communication, 47-48
  emergent social software platforms (*see* ESSPs)
  "free and easy platforms," 49-51
  open platform benefits for regulated industries, 158-160
  platforms for public communication, 48-50
  "printing press" offered by the Web, 48-49
  Twitter, 50
Web 2.0 structure
  ant colonies and the Web, 66
  attempts to categorize Web content, 58-64
  concept of irreducibility, 69
  design philosophy based on not imposing control (*see* Wikipedia)
  developers desire to avoid structure, 52
  emergent nature of the Web, 66-67
  emergent social software platforms, 69-73
  Google's approach to search, 64-66
  long-standing philosophy of efficiency from structure, 54

Web 2.0 structure (*continued*)
    purposeful absence of imposed
        structure, 54-55, 58-62
    similarities shared by current en-
        terprise systems, 53
    structure drawn from links from
        page to page, 65
    tagging and, 60-62, 67-69
    Web 1.0 belief that technology
        should impose work structures,
        52-53
    Yahoo!'s attempt to structure the
        Web's content, 58-60
Web sites, 42, 48
Wenger, Etienne, 131
Werthheimer, Michael, 183
Wikipedia
    accuracy of, 78-79
    contributor definition, 162-163
    cultural norms for interactions,
        74-75
    early structured approach,
        55-57
    founders, 55
    policies and guidelines for
        interactions, 75-78
    success of non-structured
        approach, 58
    use of tools, 74

wiki concept applied to, 57-58
wikis
    approach to version control and
        simultaneous editing, 92
    company example of use (*see*
        VistaPrint)
    concept of, 57
    ease and efficiency of use,
        94-96
    group editing uses, 130-131
    large scale application to informa-
        tion sharing (*see* Wikipedia)
    potential to have prevented 9/11,
        106-107
    usage amounts "above-the-flow,"
        184
    usage amounts "in-the-flow," 184
Williams, Ken, 31
Winer, Dave, 111
Wisdom of Crowds, The (Surowiecki)
    36, 38, 139

Y2K crisis, 5-6
Yahoo!, 58-60
Yahoo! Answers, 136

Zhu, Feng, 210

About the Author

ANDREW McAFEE studies the ways that information technology affects businesses and business as a whole. His research investigates how IT changes the way companies perform, organize themselves, and compete. In 2008 he was named by the editors of the publishing house Ziff-Davis as number 38 in their list of the "100 Most Influential People in IT." He was also named by *Baseline* magazine to a separate, unranked list of the 50 most influential people in business IT that year.

He is a principal research scientist at the MIT Sloan School's Center for Digital Business and a fellow at Harvard's Berkman Center for the Internet and Society. His blog is andrewmcafee.org/blog and his Twitter username is @amcafee. He lives in Cambridge, Massachusetts.